Living Prophecies

The Minor Prophets with Daniel and The Revelation Paraphrased

by Kenneth N. Taylor

Special Edition for

THE BILLY GRAHAM EVANGELISTIC ASSOCIATION
1300 Harmon Place, Minneapolis, Minnesota 55403

TYNDALE HOUSE, PUBLISHERS
Wheaton, Illinois

Printed in U.S.A.

First printing, April - June 1965

Second printing, July 1965

Third printing, August 1965

Fourth printing, September 1965

Fifth printing, September 1965

700,000 copies now in print.

THE BILLY GRAHAM EVANGELISTIC ASSOCIATION

1300 Harmon Place, Minneapolis, Minnesota 55403

Canada: Room 305, 414 Graham Avenue (Box 841), Winnipeg 1, Manitoba

Great Britain: Bush House, Aldwych, London, W.C. 2, England

Australia: 820 Caltex House, Sydney, New South Wales

New Zealand: Box 1040, Wellington

France: 102 Avenue des Champs-Elysee, Paris 8

Germany: Entscheidung, Postfach 16309, 6 Frankfurt 16

South America: Casilla 5055, Buenos Aires, Argentina

Introduction

Living Prophecies comes from the same translator who gave us *Living Letters* and puts the writings of the prophets into modern, easy-to-understand English.

Most of these prophets wrote about 2,500 years ago, yet their inspired writings are just as relevant to our daily lives in our increasingly dangerous and secularized age as they were to the lives of people living then. In fact, some of the prophecies are just now being fulfilled—and others are on the threshold of fulfillment!

I'm glad this volume includes *The Revelation*, a portion of Scripture too often neglected. Its translation makes this book worth its weight in gold.

One of the needs of the church today is for prophets to thunder forth, "Thus saith the Lord." In reading *Living Prophecies* my own soul has been stirred, my mind challenged, my conscience convicted, and I have rededicated my life to Jesus Christ. It is my prayer that this book will have the same effect on you!

Billy Graham

Contents

Preface

The Ancient Prophets Speak to Us Today!

Probably the prophets of ancient Israel never dreamed that the words they wrote would be read by millions 2500 years later!

Yet in these days of endless national wealth and materialism, of rising crime, bribery, divorce, drunkenness, dishonesty, murder, adultery, and general disregard for God—these are the days for reading the ancient prophets. For they lived in the same atmosphere of personal, national, and international arrogance against the God of heaven—of disregard and wilful ignorance of Him——as we do today.

Simply because these prophets were not heeded, centuries of anguish overtook the Jewish race, and an entire generation of neighboring nations disappeared from history. (Can we expect a better fate than they?)

Profit for the Taking!

The relevance of these messages to our modern situation becomes even greater when we realize that, with some exceptions, these messages were not addressed primarily to godless nations, but to the people of God: the Jewish race. And to us! For in 2 Timothy 3:16, we learn that all prophecy relates specifically to Christians: that *all* Scriptures (including *all* of the prophecies in this volume!) are profitable to *us*, teaching *us* the truths of God and His ways and His love, and pointing out the sins in *our* lives, thereby helping *us* become the godly men and women we want to be. This means that each of us, if we read these messages carefully and ask God's help in understanding them, can become the kind of person that he ought to be. Our relationship with God will be humble, strong, and joyous. What a thrilling prospect!

Don't Ignore God's Vitamins!

If this is really so—that these astounding blessings can be ours by applying to our lives the truths taught in the ancient prophecies (and the Holy Spirit says this is true), then a further startling fact is plain: that if we ignore the reading of these prophecies, our lives are subject to all sorts of ills. The vitamins provided by the Lord are being thrust aside! If your life is less than filled with joyous fruitfulness, may the reason simply be that you are not reading and acting upon these messages? *For these messages are fully as important to your spiritual growth as any other portion of the Bible, including the New Testament epistles!* Each section of the Scriptures has its special value, and can be ignored or overlooked only at great spiritual peril.

This being so, it is no happy thought to realize how few Christians in these days seem to have read the prophets more than once or twice in all their lives. And today's teen-agers in the church, apparently not at all.

The reason is clear—for the text isn't! Even mature Bible students have complained, almost bitterly, against the prophets for their long-winded, repetitious, vaguely worded (at times) and hard to understand orations. The tremendous excitement and pathos of the worst locust plague in world history (told in vivid detail in the book of *Joel*); the death of the rock-hewn city of Petra (in *Obadiah*); the story of a whole nation that wanted only jolly preachers, " 'I'll preach to you the joys of wine and drink'—that's the kind of prophet that you like!" (in *Micah*); are lost under an accurate but wordy, wooden translation!

The question is, can the accuracy be retained when the wordiness is omitted? That is what a paraphrase attempts to do. It tries to clear away from the fertile fields of Scripture the rocks and brush and rubble of literal translation, to reveal the rich soil underneath. For the richness of that soil, when placed within a soul, can produce luxuriant gardens filled with good works and faith and love. It can give birth to an understanding of the depths of God's mercy and of His awesome power and laws—laws that cannot be trifled with. Here is power and purification, just for the taking.

A Word of Caution

But before you plunge in to read, a word of caution may be needed! For after the first excitement of reading understandingly, you may be disappointed! "Is this all that Joel says?" you may feel like saying. "I thought his message would be something great, like *Philippians* or *Romans!* What's the significance of an old locust plague?"

Well, if this is your reaction, read *Joel* again—and then again and yet again until you are deeply moved by all the thrilling lessons waiting for you there. Ask the Holy Spirit's help, and He will surely give it. These prophetic books can yet become as favorite as the *Psalms,* as fruitful as the gospels, as joyous as *Philippians.* These words from God can change your life a hundred times and in a hundred different ways. He gave them to you to read and grow by. Therefore read, and grow!

Why Include "The Revelation"?

A special word should now be said about the book of *The Revelation,* and why it is included with the Old Testament prophets. First, of course, because no compilation of prophecies can be complete without it; it is one of the chief prophetic portions of the Bible.

Moreover, it sheds much light on the "end-times" mentioned so often by the other prophets. Without *The Revelation* we would be greatly limited in understanding what the older prophets were referring to in some of their allusions.

Also, *The Revelation* is included here because, as never before, now is the time for reading it. True, it is a strange book in many ways, yet it predicts more clearly than any of the other prophets the amazing events awaiting the church. Even so, it is still not to be understood in a single evening's reading. Martin Luther shook his head many times over this book. "A revelation," he complained, "should reveal!" And so it should. But not necessarily when we want it to. Much prophecy is veiled (as the angel explained to Daniel) until the time approaches for its fulfillment. Then it begins to "make sense."

And the book of *The Revelation is* beginning to

make sense today if it didn't before! For these are the days when the great prophetic theme of the rebirth of the land of Israel is being fulfilled before our eyes. Surely her "blossoming as a rose"—a blossoming predicted for the "end-times"—shows that the clock of ages is moving toward its final hour; indeed may it not even now be marking its final minutes?

Living as we do within this spirit of the end-time prophecies (if not, indeed, in their fulfillment), much that was incredible and strange in *The Revelation* has given way to a spirit of belief. Vast world populations, hydrogen bombs capable of destroying a third of the world within minutes, half the world within the grip of leaders who mock God and deny His very existence—here is shape and form and face to forces in the book of *The Revelation* that formerly were strange.

A Prayer

This book is sent out with the prayer that all who receive it will read it (and share it with their families and their friends). And that they will ask the Holy Spirit of God to open wide their spiritual eyes and hearts and understanding as they read. And that their lives will be deeply changed by the reading.

Exhortlynge instantly and besechynge those that are better sene in the tongues than I, and that have higher gifts of grace to interpret the sense of Scripture, and meaning of the Spirit, than I, to consider and ponder my labor, and that with the spirit of meekness. And if they perceive in any places that I have not attained the very sense of the tongue, or meaning of the Scripture, or have not given the right English word, that they put to their hands to amend it, remembering that so is their duty to do. For we have not received the gifts of God for ourselves only, or for to hide them; but for to bestow them unto the honoring of God and Christ and edifying of the congregation, which is the body of Christ.

—William Tyndale (1492?-1536)

(From his Prologue in the first printed English Bible)

Daniel

CHAPTER 1

Three years after King Jehoiakim began to rule in Judah, Babylon's king Nebuchadnezzar attacked Jerusalem with his armies, and the Lord gave him victory over Jehoiakim. When he returned to Babylon, he took along some of the sacred cups from the temple of God, and placed them in the treasury of his god in the land of Shinar.

3, 4 Then he ordered Ashpenaz, who was in charge of his palace personnel,* to select some of the Jewish youths brought back as captives—young men of the royal family and nobility of Judah—and to teach them the Chaldean language and literature.† "Pick strong, healthy, good-looking lads," he said; "those who have read widely in many fields, are well informed, alert and sensible, and have enough poise to look good around the palace."

5 The king assigned them the best of food and wine from his own kitchen during their three-year training period, planning to make them his counsellors when they graduated.

6 Daniel, Hananiah, Mishael, and Azariah were four of the young men chosen, all from the tribe of Judah.

7 However, their superintendent gave them Babylonian names, as follows:

*literally, "his chief eunuch." See 2 Kings 20: 17, 18.

†The language was Aramaic; the literature would have included mathematics, astronomy and history—plus a strong dose of alchemy and magic!

Daniel was called Belteshazzar;
Hananiah was called Shadrach;
Mishael was called Meshach;
Azariah was called Abednego.

8 But Daniel made up his mind not to eat the food and wine given to them by the king.* He asked the superintendent for permission to eat other things instead.†

9 Now as it happened, God had given the superintendent a special appreciation for Daniel, and sympathy for his predicament.

10 But he was alarmed by Daniel's suggestion. "I'm afraid you will become pale and thin compared with the other youths your age," he said, "and then the king will behead me for neglecting my responsibilities."

11 Daniel talked it over with the steward who was appointed by the superintendent to look after Daniel, Hananiah, Mishael, and Azariah

12 And suggested a ten-day diet of only vegetables and water;

13 Then, at the end of this trial period the steward could see how they looked in comparison with the other fellows who ate the king's rich food, and decide whether or not to let them continue their diet.

14 The steward finally agreed to the test.

15 Well, at the end of the ten days, Daniel and his three friends looked healthier and better nour-

*literally, "determined . . . that he would not defile himself." The defilement was probably in eating pork or other foods outlawed in Leviticus.

†literally, "He asked . . . to allow him not to defile himself."

ished than the youths who had been eating the food supplied by the king!

16 So after that the steward fed them only vegetables and water, without the rich foods and wines!

17 God gave these four youths great ability to learn and they soon mastered all the literature and science of the time; and God gave to Daniel special ability in understanding the meanings of dreams and visions.

18, 19 When the three-year training period was completed, the superintendent brought all the young men to the king for oral exams, as he had been ordered to do. King Nebuchadnezzar had long talks with each of them, and none of them impressed him as much as Daniel, Hananiah, Mishael, and Azariah. So they were put on his regular staff of advisors.

20 And in all matters requiring information and balanced judgment, the king found these young men's advice ten times better than that of all the skilled magicians and wise astrologers in his realm.

21 Daniel held this appointment as the king's counsellor until the first year of the reign of King Cyrus.*

CHAPTER 2

One night in the second year of his reign, Nebuchadnezzar had a terrifying nightmare, and awoke trembling with fear. And to make matters worse, he couldn't remember his dream! He immediately called in all his magicians, incantationists, sorcerers, and astrologers, and demanded that they tell him what

*So Daniel held the post at least 24 years, though perhaps intermittently, during the reigns of Nebuchadnezzar, Awel-Marduk, Neriglissar, Nabonidus, and Belshazzar.

his dream had been. "I've had a terrible nightmare," he said as they stood before him, "and I can't remember what it was. Tell me, for I fear some tragedy awaits me."

4 Then the astrologers (speaking in Aramaic) said to the king, "Sir, tell us the dream and then we can tell you what it means."

5 But the king replied, "I tell you, the dream is gone—I can't remember it. And if you won't tell me what it was and what it means, I'll have you torn limb from limb and your houses made into heaps of rubble!

6 But I will give you many wonderful gifts and honors if you tell me what the dream was and what is means. So, begin!"

7 They said again, "How can we tell you what the dream means unless you tell us what it was?"

8, 9 The king retorted, "I can see your trick! You're trying to stall for time until the calamity befalls me that the dream foretells. But if you don't tell me the dream, you certainly can't expect me to believe your interpretation!"

10 The Chaldeans replied to the king, "There isn't a man alive who can tell others what they have dreamed! And there isn't a king in all the world who would ask such a thing!

11 This is an impossible thing the king requires. No one except the gods can tell you your dream, and they are not here to help."

12 Upon hearing this, the king was furious, and sent out orders to execute all the wise men of Babylon.

13 And Daniel and his companions were rounded up with the others to be killed.

14 But when Arioch, the chief executioner, came to kill them, Daniel handled the situation with great wisdom by asking,

15 "Why is the king so angry? What is the matter?" Then Arioch told him all that had happened.

16 So Daniel went in to see the king. "Give me a little time," he said, "And I will tell you the dream and what it means."

17 Then he went home and told Hananiah, Mishael, and Azariah, his companions.

18 They asked the God of heaven to show them His mercy by telling them the secret, so they would not die with the others.

19 And that night in a vision God told Daniel what the king had dreamed. Then Daniel praised the God of heaven,

20 Saying, "Blessed be the name of God forever and ever, for He alone has all wisdom and all power.

21 World events are under His control. He removes kings and sets others on their thrones. He gives wise men their wisdom, and scholars their intelligence.

22 He reveals profound mysteries beyond man's understanding. He knows all hidden things, for He is light, and darkness is no obstacle to Him.

23 I thank and praise You, oh God of my fathers, for You have given me wisdom and glowing health, and now, even this vision of the king's dream, and the understanding of what it means."

24 Then Daniel went in to see Arioch, who had been ordered to execute the wise men of Babylon,

and said, "Don't kill them. Take me to the king and I will tell him what he wants to know."

25 Then Arioch hurried Daniel to the king and said, "I've found one of the Jewish captives who will tell you your dream!"

26 The king said to Daniel, "Is this true? Can you tell me what my dream was and what it means?"

27 Daniel replied, "No wise man, astrologer, magician, or wizard can tell the king such things,

28 But there is a God in heaven who reveals secrets, and He has told you in your dream what will happen in the future. This was your dream:

29 You dreamed of coming events. He who reveals secrets was speaking to you.

30 (But remember, it's not because I am wiser than any living person that I know this secret of your dream, for God showed it to me for your benefit.)

31 Oh king, you saw a huge and powerful statue of a man, shining brilliantly, frightening and terrible.

32 The head of the statue was made of purest gold, its chest and arms were of silver, its belly and thighs of brass,

33 Its legs of iron, its feet part iron and part clay.

34 But as you watched, a Rock was cut from the mountainside* by supernatural means. It came hurtling towards the statue and crushed the feet of iron and clay, smashing them to bits.

35 Then the whole statue collapsed into a heap of iron, clay, brass, silver, and gold; its pieces were

*implied.

crushed as small as chaff, and the wind blew them all away. But the Rock that knocked the statue down became a great mountain that covered the whole earth.

36 That was the dream; now for its meaning:

37 Your Majesty, you are a king over many kings, for the God of heaven has given you your kingdom, power, strength and glory.

38 You rule the farthest provinces, and even animals and birds are under your control, as God decreed. You are that head of gold.

39 But after your kingdom has come to an end, another world power* will arise to take your place. This empire will be inferior to yours. And after that kingdom has fallen, yet a third great power†—represented by the bronze belly of the statue—will rise to rule the world.

40 Following it, the fourth kingdom‡ will be strong as iron—smashing, bruising, and conquering.

41, 42 The feet and toes you saw—part iron and part clay—show that later on this kingdom will be divided. Some parts of it will be as strong as iron, and some as weak as clay.

43 This mixture of iron with clay also shows that these kingdoms will try to strengthen themselves by forming alliances with each other through intermarriage of their rulers; but this will not succeed, for iron and clay don't mix.

44 During the reigns of those kings, the God of heaven will set up a kingdom that will never be destroyed; no one will ever conquer it. It will shatter

*The Medo-Persian empire, whose first great ruler was Cyrus.
†The Greek empire, founded by Alexander the Great.
‡Apparently the Roman empire.

all these kingdoms into nothingness; but it shall stand forever, indestructible.

45 That is the meaning of the Rock cut from the mountain without human hands—the Rock that crushed to powder all the iron and brass, the clay, the silver, and the gold.

Thus the great God has shown what will happen in the future; and this interpretation of your dream is as sure and certain as my description of it."

46 Then Nebuchadnezzar fell to the ground before Daniel and worshiped him, and commanded his people to offer sacrifices and burn sweet incense before him.

47 "Truly, oh Daniel," the king said, "your God is the God of gods, Ruler of kings, the Revealer of mysteries, because He has told you this secret."

48 Then the king made Daniel very great; he gave him many costly gifts, and appointed him to be ruler over the whole province of Babylon, as well as chief over all his wise men.

49 Then, at Daniel's request, the king appointed Shadrach, Meshach and Abednego as Daniel's assistants, to be in charge of all the affairs of the province of Babylon; Daniel served as chief magistrate in the king's court.

CHAPTER 3

King Nebuchadnezzar made a golden statue 90 feet high and 9 feet wide and set it up on the Plain of Dura, in the province of Babylon;

2 Then he sent messages to all the princes, gov-

ernors, captains, judges, treasurers, counsellors, sheriffs, and rulers of all the provinces of his empire, to come to the dedication of his statue.

3 When they had all arrived and were standing before the monument,

4 A herald shouted out, "Oh people of all nations and languages, this is the king's command:

5 When the band* strikes up, you are to fall flat on the ground to worship King Nebuchadnezzar's golden statue;

6 Anyone who refuses to obey will immediately be thrown into a flaming furnace."

7 So when the band* began to play, everyone—whatever his nation, language, or religion†—fell to the ground and worshiped the statue.

8 But some officials went to the king and accused Daniel and his friends of refusing to worship!

9 "Your Majesty," they said to him,

10 "You made a law that everyone must fall down and worship the golden statue when the band* begins to play,

11 And that anyone who refuses will be thrown into a flaming furnace.

12 But there are some Jews out there—Shadrach, Meshach, and Abednego, whom you have put in charge of Babylonian affairs—who have defied you, refusing to serve your gods or to worship the golden statue you set up."

*literally, "the cornet, flute, harp, sackbut, psaltry, dulcimer, and every other sort of instrument."
†implied.

13 Then Nebuchadnezzar, in a terrible rage, ordered Shadrach, Meshach, and Abednego to be brought in before him.

14 "Is it true, oh Shadrach, Meshach, and Abednego," he asked, "that you are refusing to serve my gods or to worship the golden statue I set up?

15 I'll give you one more chance. When the music plays, if you fall down and worship the statue, all will be well. But if you refuse, you will be thrown into a flaming furnace within the hour. And what god can deliver you out of my hands then?"

16 Shadrach, Meshach, and Abednego replied, "Oh Nebuchadnezzar, we are not worried about what will happen to us.

17 If we are thrown into the flaming furnace, our God is able to deliver us; and He will deliver us out of your hand, Your Majesty.

18 But if He doesn't, please understand, sir, that even then we will never under any circumstance serve your gods or worship the golden statue you have erected."

19 Then Nebuchadnezzar was filled with fury and his face became dark with anger at Shadrach, Meshach, and Abednego. He commanded that the furnace be heated up seven times hotter than usual,

20 And called for some of the strongest men of his army to bind Shadrach, Meshach, and Abednego, and throw them into the fire.

21 So they bound them tight with ropes and threw them into the furnace, fully clothed.

22 And because the king, in his anger, had demanded such a hot fire in the furnace, the flames leaped out and killed the soldiers as they threw them in!

23 So Shadrach, Meshach, and Abednego fell down bound into the roaring flames.

24 But suddenly, as he was watching, Nebuchadnezzar jumped up in amazement and exclaimed to his advisors, "Didn't we throw three men into the furnace?"

"Yes," they said, "we did indeed, Your Majesty."

25 "Well, look!" Nebuchadnezzar shouted. "I see *four* men, unbound, walking around in the fire, and they aren't even hurt by the flames! And the fourth looks like a god!"*

26 Then Nebuchadnezzar came as close as he could to the open door of the flaming furnace and yelled: "Shadrach, Meshach, and Abednego, servants of the Most High God! Come out! Come here!" So they stepped out of the fire.

27 Then the princes, governors, captains, and counsellors crowded around them and saw that the fire hadn't touched them—not a hair of their heads was singed; their coats were unscorched, and they didn't even smell of smoke!

28 Then Nebuchadnezzar said, "Blessed be the God of Shadrach, Meshach, and Abednego, for He sent His angel to deliver His trusting servants when they defied the king's commandment, and were willing to die rather than serve or worship any god except their own.

29 Therefore, I make this decree, that any per-

*literally, "looks like a son of the gods."

son of any nation, language or religion* who speaks a word against the God of Shadrach, Meshach, and Abednego shall be torn limb from limb and his house knocked into a heap of rubble. For no other God can do what this One does."

30 Then the king gave promotions to Shadrach,
Meshach, and Abednego, so that they prospered
greatly there in the province of Babylon.

CHAPTER 4

This is the proclamation of Nebuchadnezzar the king, which he sent to people of every language in every nation of the world:

Greetings:

2 I want you all to know about the strange thing that the Most High God did to me.

3 It was incredible—a mighty miracle! And now I know for sure that His kingdom is everlasting; He reigns forever and ever.

4 I, Nebuchadnezzar, was living in peace and prosperity,

5 When one night I had a dream that greatly frightened me.

6 I called in all the wise men of Babylon to tell me the meaning of my dream,

7 But when they came—the magicians, astrologers, fortune tellers, and wizards—and I told them the dream, they couldn't interpret it.

8 At last Daniel came in—the man I named

*implied.

Belteshazzar after my god—the man in whom is the spirit of the holy gods, and I told him the dream.

9 "Oh Belteshazzar, master magician," I said, "I know that the spirit of the holy gods is in you and no mystery is too great for you to solve. Tell me what my dream means:

10, 11 I saw a very tall tree out in a field, growing higher and higher into the sky until it could be seen by everyone in all the world.

12 Its leaves were fresh and green, and its branches were weighted down with fruit, enough for everyone to eat. Wild animals rested beneath its shade and birds sheltered in its branches, and all the world was fed from it.

13 Then as I lay there dreaming, I saw one of God's angels* coming down from heaven.

14 He shouted, 'Cut down the tree; lop off its branches; shake off its leaves, and scatter its fruit. Get the animals out from under it and the birds from its branches,

15 But leave its stump and roots in the ground, banded with a chain of iron and brass, surrounded by the tender grass. Let the dews of heaven drench him and let him eat grass with the wild animals!

16 For seven years let him have the mind of an animal instead of a man.

17 For this has been decreed by the Watchers, demanded by the Holy Ones. The purpose of this decree is that all the world may understand that the Most High dominates the kingdoms of the

*literally, "a watcher, a holy one."

world, and gives them to anyone He wants to, even
the lowliest of men!'

18 Oh Belteshazzar, that was my dream; now tell
me what it means. For no one else can help me; all
the wisest men of my kingdom have failed me. But
you can tell me, for the spirit of the holy gods is in
you."

19 Then Daniel* sat there stunned and silent for
an hour, aghast at the meaning of the dream.
Finally the king said to him: "Belteshazzar, don't
be afraid to tell me what it means."

Daniel replied: "Oh, that the events foreshadowed in this dream would happen to your enemies, my lord, and not to you!

20 For the tree you saw growing so tall, reaching
high into the heavens for all the world to see,

21 With its fresh green leaves, loaded with fruit
for all to eat, the wild animals living in its shade,
with its branches full of birds—

22 That tree, Your Majesty, is you. For you have
grown strong and great; your greatness reaches up
to heaven, and your rule to the ends of the earth.

23 Then you saw God's angel† coming down
from heaven and saying, 'Cut down the tree and
destroy it; but leave the stump and the roots in
the earth surrounded by tender grass, banded with
a chain of iron and brass. Let him be wet with the
dew of heaven. For seven years let him eat grass
with the animals of the field.'

24 Your Majesty, the Most High God has decreed—and it will surely happen—

*literally, "Daniel, whose name was Belteshazzar."

†literally, "a holy watcher"

25 That your people will chase you from your palace, and you will live in the fields like an animal, eating grass like a cow, your back wet with dew from heaven. For seven years this will be your life, until you learn that the Most High God dominates the kingdoms of men, and gives power to anyone He chooses.

26 But the stump and the roots were left in the ground! This means that you will get your kingdom back again, when you have learned that Heaven rules.

27 Oh King Nebuchadnezzar, listen to me—stop sinning; do what you know is right; be merciful to the poor. Perhaps even yet God will spare you."

* * * *

28 But all these things happened to Nebuchadnezzar.

29 Twelve months after this dream, he was strolling on the roof of the royal palace in Babylon,

30 And saying, "I, by my own mighty power, have built this beautiful city as my royal residence, and as the capital of my empire."

31 While he was still speaking these words, a voice called down from heaven, "Oh King Nebuchadnezzar, this message is for you: You are no longer ruler of this kingdom.

32 You will be forced out of the palace to live with the animals in the fields, and to eat grass like the cows for seven years until you finally realize that God parcels out the kingdoms of men and gives them to anyone He chooses."

33 That very same hour this prophecy was fulfilled. Nebuchadnezzar was chased from his palace and ate grass like the cows, and his body was wet with dew; his hair grew as long as eagles' feathers, and his nails were like birds' claws.

* * * *

34 "At the end of seven years* I, Nebuchadnezzar, looked up to heaven, and my sanity returned, and I praised and worshiped the Most High God and honored Him who lives forever, whose rule is everlasting, His kingdom evermore.

35 All the people of the earth are nothing when compared to Him, He does whatever He thinks best among the hosts of heaven, as well as here among the inhabitants of earth. No one can stop Him or challenge Him, saying, 'What do You mean by doing these things?'

36 When my mind returned to me, so did my honor and glory and kingdom. My counsellors and officers came back to me and I was reestablished as head of my kingdom, with even greater honor than before.

37 Now I, Nebuchadnezzar, praise and glorify and honor the King of Heaven, the Judge of all, Whose every act is right and good; for He is able to take those who walk proudly and push them into the dust!"

CHAPTER 5

Belshazzar† the king invited a thousand of his officers to a great feast where the wine flowed freely.

2, 3, 4 While Belshazzar was drinking he was re-

*literally, "at the end of the days."
†See note on 1:21

minded of the gold and silver cups taken long before from the temple in Jerusalem during Nebuchadnezzar's reign, and brought to Babylon. Belshazzar
ordered that these sacred cups be brought in to the
feast; and when they arrived he and his princes,
wives, and concubines drank toasts from them to
their idols made of gold and silver, brass and iron,
wood and stone.

5 Suddenly, as they were drinking from these
cups, they saw the fingers of a man's hand writing
on the plaster of the wall opposite the lampstand.
The king himself saw the fingers as they wrote.

6 His face blanched with fear, and such terror
gripped him that his knees knocked together and
his legs gave way beneath him.

7 "Bring the magicians and astrologers!" he
screamed. "Bring the Chaldeans! Whoever reads
that writing on the wall, and tells me what it
means, will be dressed in purple robes of royal
honor with a gold chain around his neck, and become the third ruler* in the kingdom!"

8 But when they came, none of them could un-
derstand† the writing or tell him what it meant.

9 The king grew more and more hysterical; his
face reflected the terror he felt, and his officers too
were shaken.

10 But when the queen-mother heard what was
happening, she rushed to the banquet hall and said
to Belshazzar, "Calm yourself, Your Majesty, don't
be so pale and frightened over this.

11 For there is a man in your kingdom who has

*Belshazzar was the second under Nabonidus his father, who was out of town at the time.

†Since the writing was in familiar Aramaic, they could read the words but could not determine their prophetic significance.

within him the spirit of the holy gods. In the days of your father this man was found to be as full of wisdom and understanding as though he were himself a god. And in the reign of King Nebuchadnezzar,* he was made chief of all the magicians, astrologers, Chaldeans, and soothsayers of Babylon.

12 Call for this man, Daniel—or Belteshazzar, as the king called him—for his mind is filled with divine knowledge and understanding. He can interpret dreams, explain riddles, and solve knotty problems. He will tell you what the writing means."

13 So Daniel was rushed in to see the king. The king asked him, "Are you the Daniel that King Nebuchadnezzar brought from Israel as a Jewish captive?

14 I have heard that you have the spirit of the gods within you and that you are filled with enlightenment and wisdom.

15 My wise men and astrologers have tried to read that writing on the wall, and tell me what it means, but they can't.

16 I am told that you can solve all kinds of mysteries. If you can tell me the meaning of those words, I will clothe you in purple robes, with a golden chain around your neck, and make you the third ruler in the kingdom."

17 Daniel answered, "Keep your gifts, or give them to someone else; but I will tell you what they mean.

18 Your Majesty, the Most High God gave Nebuchadnezzar, who long ago preceded you, a kingdom and majesty and glory and honor.

*literally, "King Nebuchadnezzar your father"—the Aramaic word for "father" can also mean "predecessor," in this instance fifth removed.

19 He gave him such majesty that all the nations of the world trembled before him in fear. He killed any who offended him, and spared any he liked. At his whim they rose or fell.

20 But when his heart and mind were hardened in pride, God removed him from his royal throne and took away his glory,

21 And he was chased out of his palace into the fields. His thoughts and feelings became those of an animal, and he lived among the wild donkeys; he ate grass like the cows and his body was wet with the dew of heaven, until at last he knew that the Most High overrules the kingdoms of men, and that He appoints anyone He desires to reign over them.

22 And you, his successor, oh Belshazzar—you knew all this, yet you have not been humble.

23 For you have defied the Lord of Heaven, and brought here these cups from His temple; and you and your officers and wives and concubines have been drinking wine from them while praising gods of silver, gold, brass, iron, wood, and stone—gods that neither see nor hear, nor know anything at all. But you have not praised the God who gives you the breath of life and controls your destiny!

24, 25 And so God sent those fingers to write this message: *'Mene,' 'Mene,' 'Tekel,' 'Parsin.'*

26 This is what it means:

Mene means 'numbered'—God has numbered the days of your reign, and they are ended.

27 *Tekel* means 'weighed'—You have been weighed in God's balances and have failed the test.

28 *Parsin* means 'divided'—Your kingdom will be divided and given to the Medes and Persians."

29 Then at Belshazzar's command, Daniel was robed in purple, and a golden chain was hung around his neck; and he was proclaimed third ruler in the kingdom.

* * * *

30 That very night Belshazzar, the Chaldean king, was killed;

31 And Darius the Mede entered the city and began reigning at the age of sixty-two.

CHAPTER 6

Darius divided the kingdom into 120 provinces, each under a governor.

2 The governors were accountable to three presidents (Daniel was one of them) so that the king could administer the kingdom efficiently.

3 Daniel soon proved himself more capable than all the other presidents and governors, for he had great ability, and the king began to think of placing him over the entire empire as his administrative officer.

4 This made the other presidents and governors very jealous, and they began searching for some fault in the way Daniel was handling his affairs so that they could complain to the king about him. But they couldn't find anything to criticize! He was faithful and honest, and made no mistakes.

5 So they concluded, "Our only chance is his religion!"

6 They decided to go to the king and say, "King
Darius, live forever!

7 We presidents, governors, counsellors and deputies have unanimously decided that you should make a law, irrevocable under any circumstance, that for the next thirty days anyone who asks a favor of God or man—except from you, Your Majesty—shall be thrown to the lions.

8 Your Majesty, we request your signature on this law; sign it so that it cannot be canceled or changed; it will be a 'law of the Medes and Persians' that cannot be revoked."

9 So King Darius signed the law.

10 But though Daniel knew about it, he went home and knelt down as usual in his upstairs bedroom, with its windows open towards Jerusalem, and prayed three times a day, just as he always had, giving thanks to his God.

11 Then the men thronged to Daniel's house and found him praying there, asking favors of his God.

12 They rushed back to the king and reminded him about his law. "Haven't you signed a decree," they said, "that permits no petitions to any God or man—except you—for thirty days? And anyone disobeying will be thrown to the lions?"

"Yes," the king replied, "it is 'a law of the Medes and Persians', that cannot be altered or revoked."

13 Then they told the king, "That fellow, Daniel, one of the Jewish captives, is paying no attention to you or your law. He is asking favors of his God three times a day."

14 Hearing this, the king was very angry with himself for signing the law, and determined to save Daniel. He spent the rest of the day trying to think of some way to get Daniel out of this predicament.

15 In the evening the men came again to the king and said, "Your Majesty, there is nothing you can do. You signed the law and it cannot be changed."

16 So at last the king gave the order for Daniel's arrest, and he was taken to the den of lions. The king said to him, "May your God, whom you worship continually, deliver you." And then they threw him in.

17 A stone was brought and placed over the mouth of the den; and the king sealed it with his own signet ring, and that of his government, so that no one could rescue Daniel from the lions.

18 Then the king returned to his palace and went to bed without dinner. He refused his usual entertainment and didn't sleep all night.

19 Very early the next morning he hurried out to the lions' den,

20 And called out in anguish, "Oh Daniel, servant of the Living God, was your God, whom your worship continually, able to deliver you from the lions?"

21 Then he heard a voice! "Your Majesty, live forever!" It was Daniel!

22 "My God has sent His angel," he said, "to shut the lions' mouths so that they can't touch me; for I am innocent before God; nor, sir, have I wronged you."

23 The king was beside himself with joy and

ordered that Daniel be lifted from the den. And not a scratch was found on him, because he believed in his God.

24 Then the king issued a command to bring the men who had accused Daniel, and throw them into the den along with their children and wives; and the lions leaped upon them and tore them apart before they even hit the bottom of the den.

25, 26 Afterwards King Darius wrote this message addressed to everyone in his empire:

"Greetings! I decree that everyone shall tremble and fear before the God of Daniel in every part of my kingdom. For his God is the living, unchanging God whose kingdom shall never be destroyed and whose power shall never end.

27 He delivers His people, preserving them from harm; He does great miracles in heaven and earth; it is He who delivered Daniel from the power of the lions."

28 So Daniel prospered in the reign of Darius, and in the reign of Cyrus the Persian.

CHAPTER 7

One night during the first year of Belshazzar's reign over the Babylonian empire, Daniel had a dream and he wrote it down. This is his description of what he saw:

2 In my dream I saw a great storm on a mighty ocean, with strong winds blowing from every direction.

3 Then four huge animals came up out of the water, each different from the other.

4 The first was like a lion, but it had eagle's wings! And as I watched, its wings were pulled off so that it could no longer fly, and it was left standing on the ground, on two feet, like a man; and a man's mind was given to it.

5 The second animal looked like a bear with its paw raised, ready to strike. It held three ribs between its teeth, and I heard a voice saying to it, "Get up! Devour many people!"

6 The third of these strange animals looked like a leopard, but it had on its back wings like those of birds; and it had four heads! And great power was given to it over all mankind.

7 Then, as I watched in my dream, a fourth animal rose up out of the ocean, too dreadful to describe and incredibly strong. It devoured some of its victims by tearing them apart with its huge iron teeth; and others it crushed beneath its feet. It was far more brutal and vicious than any of the other animals, and it had ten horns.

8 As I was looking at the horns, suddenly another small horn appeared among them, and three of the first ones were yanked out, roots and all, to give it room; this little horn had a man's eyes and a bragging mouth.

9 I watched as thrones were put in place and the Ancient of Days—the Almighty God—sat down to judge. His clothing was as white as snow, His hair like whitest wool. He sat upon a fiery throne brought in on flaming wheels, and

[10] A river of fire flowed from before Him. Millions of angels ministered to Him and hundreds of millions of people stood before Him waiting to be judged. Then the court began its session and The Books were opened.

[11] As I watched, the brutal fourth animal was killed and its body handed over to be burned because of its arrogance against Almighty God, and the boasting of its little horn.

[12] As for the other three animals, their kingdoms were taken from them, but they were allowed to live a short time longer.*

[13] Next I saw the arrival of a Man—or so He seemed to be—brought there on clouds from heaven; He approached the Ancient of Days and was presented to Him.

[14] He was given the ruling power and glory over all the nations of the world, so that all people of every language must obey Him. His power is eternal —it will never end; His government shall never fall.

[15] I was confused and disturbed by all I had seen (Daniel wrote in his report),

[16] So I approached one of those standing beside the throne and asked him the meaning of all these things, and he explained them to me.

[17] "These four huge animals," he said, "represent four kings who will someday rule the earth.

[18] But in the end the people of the Most High God shall rule the governments of the world forever and forever."

*literally, "for a season and a time."

[19] Then I asked about the fourth animal, the
one so brutal and shocking, with its iron teeth and
brass claws that tore men apart and that stamped
others to death with its feet.
[20] I asked, too, about the ten horns and the
little horn that came up afterwards and destroyed
three of the others—the horn with the eyes, and
the loud, bragging mouth, and was stronger than
the others.
[21] For I had seen this horn warring against God's
people and winning,
[22] Until the Ancient of Days came and opened
His court and vindicated His people, giving them
worldwide powers of government.
[23] "This fourth animal," he told me, "is the
fourth world power* that will rule the earth. It will
be more brutal than any of the others; it will devour the whole world, destroying everything before
it.
[24] His ten horns are ten kings that will rise out
of his empire; then another king† will arise more
brutal than the other ten, and will destroy three of
them.
[25] He will defy the Most High God, and wear
down the saints with persecution, and try to change
all laws, morals and customs.‡ God's people will be
helpless in his hands for 3½ years.
[26] But then the Ancient of Days will come§ and
open His court of justice and take all power from
this vicious king, to consume and destroy it until
the end.
[27] Then every nation under heaven, and all their

*Usually believed to be a revived Roman Empire. See 2:40.
†Probably the future Antichrist of 2 Thessalonians 2:3, 4.
‡literally, "change the times and the law." Perhaps the meaning is, "change right to wrong and wrong to right."
§implied from verse 22.

power, shall be given to the people of God;* they shall rule all things forever, and all rulers shall serve and obey them."

28 That was the end of the dream. When I awoke, I was greatly disturbed, and my face was pale with fright, but I told no one what I had seen.

CHAPTER 8

In the third year of the reign of King Belshazzar, I had another dream similar to the first.

2 This time I was at Susa, the capital,† in the province of Elam, standing beside the Ulai River.

3 As I was looking around, I saw a ram with two long horns standing on the river bank; and as I watched, one of these horns began to grow, so that it was longer than the other.

4 The ram butted everything out of its way and no one could stand against it or help its victims. It did as it pleased and became very great.

5 While I was wondering what this could mean, suddenly a buck goat appeared from the west, so swiftly that it didn't even touch the ground. This goat, which had one very large horn between its eyes,

6 Rushed furiously at the two-horned ram.

7 And the closer he came, the angrier he was. He charged into the ram and broke off both his horns. Now the ram was helpless and the buck goat knocked him down and trampled on him, for there was no one to rescue him.

*literally, "the people of the saints of the Most High."
†Susa was one of several capitals of the empire at this time.

8 The victor became both proud and powerful,
but suddenly, at the height of his power, his horn
was broken; and in its place grew four good-sized
horns* pointing in four directions.
9 One of these, growing slowly at first, soon became very strong and attacked the south and east,
and warred against the land of Israel.†
10 He fought against the people of God‡ and defeated some of their leaders.‡
11 He even challenged the Commander§ of the
army of heaven by canceling the daily sacrifices offered to Him, and by defiling His temple.
12 But the army of heaven was restrained from
destroying him for this transgression. As a result,
truth and righteousness perished, and evil tri-
umphed and prospered.**
13 Then I heard two of the holy angels talking to
each other. One of them said, "How long will it be
until the daily sacrifice is restored again? How long
until the destruction of the temple is avenged and
God's people triumph?"
14 The other replied, "1150 days†† must first go
by."
15 As I was trying to understand the meaning of
this vision, suddenly a man was standing in front
of me—or at least he looked like a man—

*The four principal successors of Alexander the Great were Ptolemy I of Egypt, Seleucus of Babylonia, Antigonus of Syria and Asia Minor, and Antipater of Macedonia and Greece.

†literally, "the glorious land." Israel was attacked by Antiochus IV Epiphanes, with a further fulfillment of this prophecy indicated for the future; see verses 17, 19, 23.

‡literally, "host of heaven" and "the starry host." See 8:24.

§compare Joshua 5:13-15.

**or, "And great indignities were perpetrated against the temple ceremonies, so truth and righteousness perished." The Hebrew text is obscure.

††literally, "2300 mornings and evenings," about 3½ years.

16 And I heard a man's voice calling from across the river, "Gabriel, tell Daniel the meaning of his dream."

17 So Gabriel started toward me. But as he approached, I was too frightened to stand, and fell down with my face to the ground. "Son of man," he said, "you must understand that the events you have seen in your vision will not take place until the end times come."

18 Then I fainted, lying face downward on the ground. But he roused me with a touch, and helped me to my feet.

19 "I am here," he said, "to tell you what is going to happen in the last days of the coming time of terror—for what you have seen pertains to that final event in history.

20 The two horns of the ram you saw are the kings of Media and Persia,

21 The shaggy-haired goat is the nation of Greece; and its long horn represents the first great king of that country.

22 When you saw the horn break off, and four smaller horns replacing it, this means that the Grecian empire will break into four sections with four kings, none of them as great as the first.

23 Toward the end of their kingdoms, when they have become morally rotten, an angry king shall rise to power with great shrewdness and intelligence.*

24 His power shall be mighty, but it will be satanic† strength and not his own. Prospering

*literally, "one who understands riddles"; an alternate rendering might read, "skilled in intrigues." Probably a reference to Antiochus Epiphanes and future further fulfillment by the Antichrist at the end of human history.

†implied. Literally, "but not with his power."

wherever he turns, he will destroy all who oppose him, though their armies be mighty; and he will devastate God's people.

25 He will be a master of deception, defeating many by catching them off guard as they bask in false security. Without warning he will destroy them. So great will he fancy himself to be that he will even take on the Prince of Princes in battle; but in so doing he will seal his own doom, for he shall be broken by the hand of God, though no human means could overpower him.

26 And then in your vision you heard about the 1150 days to pass before the rights of worship are restored. This number is literal, and means just that.* But none of these things will happen for a long time, so don't tell anyone about them yet."

27 Then I grew faint and was sick for several days. Afterwards I was up and around again and performed my duties for the king, but I was greatly distressed by the dream and did not understand it.

CHAPTER 9

It was now the first year of the reign of King Darius, the son of Ahasuerus. (Darius was a Mede but became king of the Chaldeans.)

2 In that first year of his reign I, Daniel, learned from the book of Jeremiah the prophet, that Jerusalem must lie desolate for 70 years.†

3 So I earnestly pleaded with the Lord God (to

*literally, "The vision of the evenings and the mornings which has been told is true." Verse 14 is the basis for the meaning expressed in the paraphrase.

†Jeremiah 25:11-12; 29:10. This interval had now almost expired.

end our captivity and send us back to our own land).* As I prayed, I fasted, and wore rough sackcloth, and sprinkled myself with ashes,

4 And confessed my sins and those of my people. "Oh Lord," I prayed, "You are a great and awesome God; You always fulfill Your promises of mercy to those who love You and who keep Your laws.

5 But we have sinned so much; we have rebelled against You and scorned Your commands.

6 We have refused to listen to Your servants the prophets, whom You sent again and again down through the years, with Your messages to our kings and princes and to all the people.

7 Oh Lord, You are righteous; but as for us, we are always shame-faced with sin, just as You see us now; yes, all of us—the men of Judah, the people of Jerusalem, and all Israel, scattered near and far wherever You have driven us because of our disloyalty to You.

8 Oh Lord, we and our kings and princes and fathers are weighted down with shame because of all our sins.

9 But the Lord our God is merciful, and pardons even those who have rebelled against Him.

10 Oh Lord our God we have disobeyed You; we have flouted all the laws You gave us through Your servants, the prophets.

11 All Israel has disobeyed; we have turned away from You and haven't listened to Your voice. And so the awesome curse of God has crushed us—the curse written in the law of Moses Your servant.

*implied.

12 And You have done exactly as You warned us
You would do; for never in all history has there
been a disaster like what happened at Jerusalem to
us and our rulers.
13 Every curse against us written in the law of
Moses has come true; all the evils he predicted—all
have come. But even so we still refuse to satisfy the
Lord our God by turning from our sins and doing
right.
14 And so the Lord deliberately crushed us with
the calamity He prepared; He is fair in everything
He does, but we would not obey.
15 Oh Lord our God, You brought lasting honor
to Your Name by removing Your people from
Egypt in a great display of power. Lord, do it again!
Though we have sinned so much and are full of
wickedness,
16 Yet because of all Your faithful mercies, Lord,
please turn away Your furious anger from Jerusalem, Your own city, Your holy mountain. For the
heathen mock at You because Your city lies in
ruins for our sins.
17 Oh our God, hear Your servant's prayer!
Listen as I plead! Let Your face shine again with
peace and joy upon Your desolate sanctuary—for
Your own glory, Lord.
18 Oh my God, bend down Your ear and listen to
my plea. Open Your eyes and see our wretchedness;
how Your city lies in ruins—for everyone knows
that it is Yours. We don't ask because we merit
help, but because You are so merciful despite our
grievous sins.
19 Oh Lord, hear; oh Lord, forgive. Oh Lord,
listen to me and act! Don't delay—for Your own

sake, oh my God; because Your people and Your
city bear Your name."
20 Even while I was praying and confessing my
sin and the sins of my people, and desperately
pleading with the Lord my God for Jerusalem, His
holy mountain,
21 Gabriel, whom I had seen in the earlier vision,
flew swiftly to me at the time of the evening sacrifice,
22 And said to me, "Daniel, I am here to help you
understand God's plans.
23 The moment you began praying, a command
was given. I am here to tell you what it was, for
God loves you very much. Listen, and try to understand the meaning of the vision that you saw!
24 The Lord has commanded 490 years* of
further punishment upon Jerusalem and your
people. Then at last they will learn to stay away
from sin, and their guilt will be cleansed; then the
kingdom of everlasting righteousness will begin,
and the Most Holy Place (in the temple) will be
rededicated, as the prophets have declared.
25 Now listen! It will be 49 years plus 434 years†
from the time the command is given to rebuild
Jerusalem, until the Anointed One comes! Jerusalem's streets and walls will be rebuilt despite the
perilous times.
26 After this period of 434 years, the Anointed
One will be killed, His kingdom still unrealized . . .
and a king will arise whose armies will destroy the

*literally, "70 weeks" or "70 sevens" (of years). These were not in uninterrupted sequence. See verses 25-27.

†This totals 483 years, instead of the 490 years mentioned in verse 24, leaving 7 years unaccounted for at the time of Messiah's death. For their future fulfillment see verse 27 and The Revelation. Or, consider the destruction of Jerusalem in A.D. 70 by Titus and the subsequent slaughter of 1,000,000 Jews during the following 3½ years as at least a partial fulfillment of this prophecy.

city and the temple. They will be overwhelmed as with a flood, and war and its miseries are decreed from that time to the very end.

27 This king will make a seven-year treaty with the people, but after half that time, he will break his pledge and stop the Jews from all their sacrifices and their offerings; then, as a climax to all his terrible deeds, the Enemy shall utterly defile the sanctuary of God. But in God's time and plan, His judgment will be poured out upon this Evil One."

CHAPTER 10

In the third year of the reign of Cyrus, king of Persia, Daniel (also called Belteshazzar) had another vision. It concerned events certain to happen in the future: times of great tribulation—wars and sorrows; and this time he understood what the vision meant.

2 When this vision came to me (Daniel said later) I had been in mourning for three full weeks.

3 All that time I tasted neither wine nor meat; and of course I went without desserts; I neither washed nor shaved nor combed my hair.

4 Then one day early in April, as I was standing beside the great Tigris River,

5, 6 I looked up and suddenly there before me stood a person robed in linen garments, with a belt of purest gold around his waist and glowing, lustrous skin! From his face came blinding flashes like lightning, and his eyes were pools of fire; his arms and feet shown like polished brass, and his voice was like the roaring of a vast multitude of people.

7 I, Daniel, alone saw this great vision; the men with me saw nothing; but they were suddenly filled with unreasoning terror and ran to hide,

8 And I was left alone. When I saw this fearful vision my strength left me; and I grew pale and weak with fright.

9 Then he spoke to me, and I fell to the ground face downward in a deep faint.

10 But a hand touched me and lifted me, still trembling, to my hands and knees.

11 And I heard his voice—"Oh Daniel, greatly beloved of God," he said, "stand up and listen carefully to what I have to say to you, for God has sent me to you." So I stood up, still trembling with fear.

12 Then he said, "Don't be frightened, Daniel, for your request has been heard in heaven and was answered the very first day you began to fast before the Lord and pray for understanding; that very day I was sent here to meet you.

13 But for 21 days the mighty Evil Spirit who overrules the kingdom of Persia* blocked my way. Then Michael, one of the top officers of the heavenly army, came to help me, so that I was able to break through these spirit rulers of Persia.

14 Now I am here to tell you what will happen to your people, the Jews, at the end times—for the fulfillment of this prophecy is many years away."

*literally, "the prince of Persia."

15 All this time I was looking down, unable to
speak a word.

16 Then someone—he looked like a man—
touched my lips and I could talk again; and I said
to the messenger from heaven, "Sir, I am terrified
by your appearance and have no strength.

17 How can such a person as I even talk to you?
For my strength is gone and I can hardly breathe."

18 Then the one who seemed to be a man touched
me again, and I felt my strength returning.

19 "God loves you very much," he said; "don't
be afraid! Calm yourself; be strong—yes, strong!"
Suddenly, as he spoke these words, I felt stronger
and said to him, "Now you can go ahead and speak,
sir, for you have strengthened me."

20, 21 He replied, "Do you know why I have
come? I am here to tell you what is written in the
Book of the Future. Then, when I leave, I will go
again to fight my way back, past the prince of
Persia; and after him, the prince of Greece. Only
Michael, the angel who guards your people Israel,*
will be there to help me."

CHAPTER 11

I was the one sent to strengthen and help Darius
the Mede in the first year of his reign.

2 But now I will show you what the future holds.
Three more Persian kings will reign, to be succeed-
ed by a fourth,† far richer than the others. Using
his wealth for political advantage, he will plan total
war against Greece.

*literally, "your prince."
†Perhaps Xerxes (486-465) who launched an all-out effort against Greece.

3 Then a mighty king will rise in Greece, a king who will rule a vast kingdom and accomplish everything he sets out to do.*

4 But at the zenith of his power, his kingdom will break apart and be divided into four weaker nations, not even ruled by his sons. For his empire will be torn apart and given to others.

5 One of them, the king of Egypt,† will increase in power, but this king's own officials will rebel against him and take away his kingdom and make it still more powerful.

6 Several years later an alliance will be formed between the king of Syria‡ and the king of Egypt. The daughter of the king of Egypt will be given in marriage to the king of Syria as a gesture of peace;§ but she will lose her influence over him and not only will her hopes be blighted, but those of her father, the king of Egypt, and of her ambassador and child.

7 But when her brother** takes over as king of Egypt, he will raise an army against the king of Syria, and march against him and defeat him.

8 When he returns again to Egypt he will carry back their idols with him, along with priceless gold and silver dishes and for many years afterwards he will leave the Syrian king alone;

*Doubtless Alexander the Great.

†literally, "the southern king"—Ptolemy II.

‡literally, "the king of the north," and so also throughout this passage. These prophecies seem to have been fulfilled many years later in the Seleucid wars between Egypt and Syria.

§In 252 B.C. Ptolemy II of Egypt gave his daughter Berenice in marriage to Antiochus II of Syria to conclude a treaty of peace between their two lands.

**literally, "from a branch." Berenice, murdered in Antioch by Antiochus II's former wife Laodice, was the sister of Ptolemy III who now ascended the Egyptian throne and declared war against the Seleucids to avenge his sister's murder.

9 Meanwhile the king of Syria* will invade Egypt briefly, but will soon return again to his own land.

10, 11 However, the sons of this Syrian king will assemble a mighty army that will overflow across Israel into Egypt, to a fortress there. Then the king of Egypt† in great anger, will rally against the vast forces of Syria and defeat them.

12 Filled with pride after this great victory, he will have many thousands of his enemies killed, but his success will be short-lived.

13 A few years later the Syrian king‡ will return with a fully-equipped army far greater than the one he lost,

14 And other nations will join him in a crusade against Egypt. Insurgents among your own people, the Jews, will join them, thus fulfilling prophecy,§ but they will not succeed.

15 Then the Syrian king and his allies will come and lay siege to a fortified city of Egypt and capture it, and the proud armies of Egypt will go down to defeat.

16 The Syrian king will march onward unopposed; none will be able to stop him. And he will also enter 'The Glorious Land' of Israel, and pillage it.

17 This will be his plot for conquering all Egypt: he too will form an alliance with the Egyptian king, giving him a daughter in marriage, so that she can work for him from within. But the plan will fail.

18 After this he will turn his attention to the

*Seleucus II
†Ptolemy IV
‡Possibly Antiochus III the Great, who was later defeated by the Romans at Magnesia. Compare verse 18.
§literally, "in order to fulfill the vision."

coastal cities and conquer many. But a general will
stop him and cause him to retreat in shame.
19 He will turn homeward again, but will have
trouble on the way, and disappear.
20 His successor* will be remembered as the king
who sent a tax collector into Israel, but after a
very brief reign, he will die mysteriously, neither in
battle nor in riot.
21 Next to come to power will be an evil man not
directly in line for royal succession.† But during
a crisis he will take over the kingdom by flattery
and intrigue.
22 Then all opposition will be swept away before
him, including a leader of the priests.‡
23 His promises will be worthless. From the first
his method will be deceit; with a mere handful of
followers, he will become strong.
24 He will enter the richest areas of the land
without warning and do something never done before: he will take the property and wealth of the
rich and scatter it out among the people. With
great success he will besiege and capture powerful
strongholds throughout his dominions, but this will
last for only a short while.
25 Then he will stir up his courage and raise a
great army against Egypt; and Egypt, too, will
raise a mighty army, but to no avail, for plots
against him will succeed.
26 Those of his own household will bring his
downfall; his army will desert, and many be killed.
27 Both these kings§ will be plotting against each

*Seleucus IV, successor of Antiochus III, sent Heliodorus to rob and desecrate the temple in Jerusalem.

†This may refer to Antiochus IV Epiphanes who, when his brother Seleucus was assassinated, ingratiated himself with the Romans and took over.

‡Probably Jason, treacherously removed by the Hellenist Menelaus.

§Probably Antiochus IV and Ptolemy IV.

other at the conference table, attempting to deceive each other. But it will make no difference, for neither can succeed until God's appointed time has come.

28 The Syrian king will then return home with great riches, first marching through Israel and destroying it.

29 Then, at the predestined time, he will once again turn his armies southward, as he had threatened, but now it will be a very different story from those first two occasions.

30, 31 For Roman warships* will scare him off, and he will withdraw and return home. Angered by having to retreat, the Syrian king will again pillage Jerusalem and pollute the sanctuary,† putting a stop to the daily sacrifices, and worshiping idols inside the temple.‡ He will leave godless Jews in power when he leaves—men who have abandoned their fathers' faith.

32 He will flatter those who hate the things of God,§ and win them over to his side. But the people who know their God** shall be strong and do great things.

33 Those with spiritual understanding will have a wide ministry of teaching in those days. But they will be in constant danger, many of them dying by fire and sword, or being jailed and robbed.

34 Eventually these pressures will subside, and some ungodly men will come, pretending to offer a helping hand, only to take advantage of them.

35 And some who are most gifted in the things

*or, from Cyprus.
†by offering swine on the altar. This event was fulfilled in 168-167 B.C.
‡literally, "they shall set up the abomination that astonished."
§Menelaus, the high priest, who conspired with Antiochus against the Jews who were loyal to God's laws.
**perhaps the valiant Maccabees and their sympathizers. But a further fulfillment may lie in the future.

of God will stumble in those days and fall, but this will only refine and cleanse them and make them pure until the final end of all their trials, at God's appointed time.

36 The king will do exactly as he pleases, claiming to be greater than every god there is, even blaspheming the God of gods, and prospering—until his time is up. For God's plans are unshakable.

37 He will have no regard for the gods of his fathers, nor for the god beloved of women,* nor any other god, for he will boast that he is greater than them all.

38 Instead of these he will worship the Fortress god†—a god his fathers never knew—and lavish on him costly gifts!

39 Claiming his help he will have great success against the strongest fortresses. He will honor those who submit to him, appointing them to positions of authority, and dividing the land to them as their reward.

40 Then at the time of the end,‡ the king of the south will attack him again, and the northern king will react with the strength and fury of a whirlwind; his vast army and navy will rush out to bury him with their might.

41 He will invade various lands on the way, including Israel, the Pleasant Land; and overthrow the governments of many nations. Moab, Edom, and most of Ammon will escape,

42 But Egypt and many other lands will be occupied.

*See Ezekiel 18:14. Tammuz-Adonis, a Babylonian god.
†literally, "the god of Fortresses."
‡The prophecy takes a turn here. Antiochus IV fades from view and the Antichrist of the last days becomes the center of attention from this point on.

43 He will capture all the treasures of Egypt, and
the Libyans and Ethiopians shall be his servants.
44 But then news from the east and north will
alarm him and he will return in great anger to
destroy as he goes.
45 He will halt between Jerusalem and the sea,
and there pitch his royal tents, but while he is there
his time will suddenly run out and there will be no
one to help him."

CHAPTER 12

At that time Michael, the mighty angelic prince
who stands guard over your nation, will stand up
(and fight for you in heaven against satanic
forces);* and there will be a time of anguish for the
Jews greater than any previous suffering in Jewish
history. And yet every one of your people whose
names are written in the Book will endure it.
2 And many of those whose bodies lie dead and
buried will rise up, some to everlasting life and some
to shame and everlasting contempt.
3 And those who are wise—the people of God—
shall shine as brightly as the sun's brilliance; and
those who turn many to righteousness will glitter
like stars forever.
4 But Daniel, keep this prophecy a secret; seal it
up so that it will not be understood until the end
times, when travel and education shall be vastly
increased!"
5 Then I, Daniel, looked and saw two men† on
each bank of a river.
6 And one of them asked the man in linen robes

*implied.
†Hebrew: "two others," probably angels.

who was standing now above the river, "How long
will it be until all these terrors end?"

7 He replied, with both hands lifted to heaven,
taking oath by Him who lives forever and ever, that
they will not end until 3½ years* after the power
of God's people has been crushed.

8 I heard what he said but I didn't understand
what he meant, so I said, "Sir, how will this all
come out?"

9 But he said, "Go now, Daniel, for what I have
said is not to be understood until the time of the
end.

10 Many shall be purified by great trials and
persecutions. But the wicked shall continue in their
wickedness, and none of them will understand.
Only those who are willing to learn will know what
it means.

11 From the time the daily sacrifice is taken away
and the Horrible Thing is set up to be worshiped,
there will be 1,290 days.†

12 And blessed are those who wait and remain
until the 1335th day!

13 But go on now to the end of your life and your
rest; for you will rise again and have your full share
of those last days."‡

*literally, "a time, times, and half a time . . . when the shattering of the power of the holy people comes to an end."
†3½ years (verse 7) plus 1 month.
‡literally, "at the end of the days."

Hosea

CHAPTER 1

These are the messages from the Lord to Hosea, son of Beeri, during the reigns of these four kings of Judah:

Uzziah,
Jotham,
Ahaz, and
Hezekiah;

and one of the kings of Israel, Jeroboam, son of Joash.

2 Here is the first message:

The Lord said to Hosea, "Go and marry a girl who is a prostitute, so that some of her children will be born to you from other men. This will illustrate the way My people have been untrue to Me, committing open adultery against Me by worshiping other gods."

3 So Hosea married Gomer, daughter of Diblaim, and she conceived and bore him a son.

4, 5 And the Lord said, "Name the child Jezreel, for in the Valley of Jezreel I am about to punish King Jehu's dynasty to avenge the murders* he committed; in fact, I will put an end to Israel as an independent kingdom, breaking the power of the nation in the Valley of Jezreel."†

6 Soon Gomer had another child—this one a

*He went far beyond God's command to execute the family of Ahab. See 1 Kings 21:21 and 2 Kings 10:11.
†A prediction of the Assyrian conquest of Israel 25 years later.

daughter. And God said to Hosea, "Name her
Lo-Ruhamah (meaning 'no more mercy') for I will
have no more mercy upon Israel, to forgive her
again.
7 But I *will* have mercy on the tribe of Judah. I
will personally free her from her enemies without
any help from her armies or her weapons."*
8 After Gomer had weaned Lo-Ruhamah, she
again conceived and this time gave birth to a son.
9 And God said, "Call him Lo-Ammi (meaning
'not mine'), for Israel is not Mine and I am not
her God.
10 Yet the time will come when Israel shall prosper and become a great nation; in that day her
people will be too numerous to count—like sand
along a seashore! Then, instead of saying to them,
'You are not My people,' I will tell them, 'You are
My sons, children of the Living God.'
11 Then the people of Judah and Israel will unite
and have one leader; they will return from exile together; what a day that will be—the day when God
will sow His people in the fertile soil of their own
land again.†

CHAPTER 2

Oh Jezreel,‡ rename your brother and sister.
Call your brother Ammi (which means "Now you
are mine"); name your sister Ruhamah ("Pitied"),
for now God will have mercy upon her!
2 Plead with your mother; for she has become

*Soon after defeating Israel, the Assyrian Emperor Sennacherib invaded Judah and besieged Jerusalem. He was driven off by special intervention of God's angel (Isaiah 36-37).

†literally, "the day of Jezreel ('God Sows')" see 2:23.

‡"Jezreel" is implied from the preceding chapter and verse.

another man's wife—I am no longer her husband.
Beg her to stop her harlotry, to quit giving herself
to others.
3 If she doesn't, I will strip her as naked as the
day she was born, and cause her to waste away and
die of thirst as in a land riddled with famine and
drought.
4 And I will not give special favors to her children as I would to my own, for they are not my
children; they belong to other men.
5 For their mother has committed adultery. She
did a shameful thing when she said, "I'll run after
other men and sell myself to them for food and
drinks and clothes."
6 But I will fence her in with briars and thorn-
bushes; I'll block the road before her to make her
lose her way, so that
7 When she runs after her lovers she will not
catch up with them. She will search for them but
not find them. Then she will think, "I might as
well return to my husband, for I was better off with
Him than I am now."
8 She doesn't realize that all she has, has come
from Me. It was I who gave her all the gold and
silver that she used in worshiping Baal, her god!
9 But now I will take back the wine and ripened
corn I constantly supplied, and the clothes I gave
her to cover her nakedness—I will no longer give
her rich harvests of grain in its season, or wine at
the time of the grape harvest.
10 Now I will expose her nakedness in public for
all her lovers to see, and no one will be able to
rescue her from My hand.
11 I will put an end to all her joys, her parties,
holidays and feasts.

12 I will destroy her vineyards and her orchards—
gifts she claims her lovers gave her—and let them
grow into a jungle; wild animals will eat their fruit.

13 For all the incense that she burned to Baal her
idol and for the times when she put on her earrings
and jewels and went out looking for her lovers, and
deserted Me: for all these things I will punish her,"
says the Lord.

* * * *

14 But I will court her again, and bring her into
the wilderness, and speak to her tenderly there.

15 There I will give back her vineyards to her,
and transform her Valley of Troubles into a Door
of Hope. She will respond to me there, singing with
joy as in days long ago in her youth, after I had
freed her from captivity in Egypt.

16 In that coming day, says the Lord, she will
call me "My Husband" instead of "My Master."*

17 Oh Israel, I will cause you to forget your idols,
and their names will not be spoken any more.

18 At that time I will make a treaty between you
and the wild animals, birds and snakes, not to fear
each other any more; and I will destroy all weapons,
and all wars will end. Then you will lie down in
peace and safety, unafraid;

19 And I will bind you to Me forever with chains
of righteousness and justice and love and mercy.

*literally, "my Baal," meaning "my Lord," but this was a tainted word because applied to idols, so it will no longer be used in reference to the true God.

[20] I will betroth you to Me in faithfulness and love, and you will really know Me then as you never have before.

[21, 22] In that day, says the Lord, I will answer the pleading of the sky for clouds, to pour down water on the earth in answer to its cry for rain. Then the earth can answer the parched cry of the grain, the grapes, and the olive trees for moisture and for dew—and the whole grand chorus shall sing together that "God sows!"* He has given all!

[23] At that time I will sow a crop of Israelites and raise them for Myself! I will pity those who are "not pitied,"† and I will say to those who are "not My people," "Now you are My people"; and they will reply, "You are our God!"

CHAPTER 3

Then the Lord said to me, "Go, and get your wife again and bring her back to you and love her, even though she loves adultery. For the Lord still loves Israel though she has turned to other gods and offered them choice gifts."

[2] So I bought her (back from her slavery),‡ for a couple of dollars and eight bushels of barley,

[3] And I said to her, "You must live alone for many days; do not go out with other men nor be a harlot; and I will wait for you."

[4] This illustrates the fact that Israel will be a

*literally, "Jezreel."
†See chapter 1, verses 6, 9, and 10.
‡implied.

long time without a king or prince; and without an
altar, temple, priests, or even idols!

5 Afterwards they will return to the Lord their
God, and to the Messiah, their king;* and they
shall come trembling, submissive to the Lord and
to His blessings, in the end times.

CHAPTER 4

Hear the word of the Lord, oh people of Israel.
The Lord has filed a lawsuit against you listing
the following charges: There is no faithfulness, no
kindness, no knowledge of God in your land.

2 You swear and lie and kill and steal and commit adultery. There is violence everywhere, with
one murder after another.

3 That is why your land is not producing; it is
filled with sadness, and all living things grow sick
and die; the animals, the birds, and even the fish
begin to disappear.

4 Don't point your finger at someone else, and
try to pass the blame to him! Look, priest, I am
pointing My finger at *you*.

5 As a sentence for your crimes, you priests will
stumble in broad daylight as well as in the night;
and so will your false "prophets" too; and I will
destroy your mother, Israel.

6 My people are destroyed because they don't
know Me; and it is all your fault, you priests, for

*literally, "to David, their king." Christ was "the greater David."

you yourselves refuse to know Me; therefore I refuse to recognize you as My priests. Since you have forgotten My laws, I will "forget" to bless your children.

7 The more My people multiplied, the more they sinned against Me. They exchanged the glory of God for the disgrace of idols.

8 The priests rejoice in the sins of the people; they lap it up and lick their lips for more!

9 And thus it is: "Like priest, like people"—because the priests are wicked, the people are too. Therefore, I will punish both priests and people for all their wicked deeds.

10 They will eat and still be hungry. Though they do a big business as prostitutes, they shall have no children, for they have deserted Me and turned to other gods.

11 Wine, women, and song have robbed My people of their brains.

12 For they are asking a piece of wood to tell them what to do. "Divine Truth" comes to them through tea leaves!* Longing after idols has made them foolish. For they have played the harlot, serving other gods, deserting Me.

13 They sacrifice to idols on the tops of mountains; they go up into the hills to burn incense beneath the pleasant shade of oaks and poplars and terebinth trees. There your daughters turn to prostitution and your brides commit adultery.

*literally, "their staff." There is no modern parallel to this ancient practice used by sorcerers, whose predictions were based on how their staffs landed on the ground when thrown or allowed to fall.

[14] But why should I punish them? For you men
are doing the same thing, sinning with harlots and
temple prostitutes. Fools! Your doom is sealed,
for you refuse to understand.
[15] But though Israel is a prostitute, may Judah
stay far from such a life. Oh Judah, do not join
with those who insincerely worship me at Gilgal and
at Bethel. Their worship is a mere pretense.
[16] Don't be like Israel, stubborn as a heifer, resisting the Lord's attempts to lead her in green
pastures.
[17] Stay away from her, for she is wedded to
idolatry.
[18] The men of Israel finish up their drinking
bouts, and off they go to find some whores. Their
love for shame is greater than for honor.*
[19] Therefore, a mighty wind† shall sweep them
away; they shall die in shame, because they sacrifice
to idols.

CHAPTER 5

Listen to this, you priests and all of Israel's leaders; listen, all you men of the royal family: You are
doomed! For you have deluded the people with
idols at Mizpah and Tabor,
[2] And dug a deep pit to trap them at Acacia.
But never forget—I will settle up with all of you
for what you've done.
[3] I have seen your evil deeds: Israel, you have
left Me as an harlot does her husband; you are
utterly defiled.

*The Hebrew text is uncertain. This translation follows the Greek version.
†The Assyrian invasion came about 20 years later and the nation disappeared.

4 Your deeds won't let you come to God again; for the spirit of adultery is deep within you, and you cannot know the Lord.

5 The very arrogance of Israel testifies against her in My court. She will stumble under her load of guilt, and Judah, too, shall fall.

6 Then at last, they will come with their flocks and herds to sacrifice to God, but it will be too late—they will not find Him. He has withdrawn from them and they are left alone.

7 For they have betrayed the honor of the Lord, bearing children that aren't His. Suddenly they and all their wealth will disappear.

8 Sound the alarm! Warn with trumpet blasts in Gibeah and Ramah, and on over to Bethaven; tremble, land of Benjamin!

9 Hear this announcement, Israel: When your day of punishment comes, you will become a heap of rubble.

10 The leaders of Judah have become the lowest sort of thieves.* Therefore, I will pour My anger down upon them like a waterfall;

11 And Ephraim will be crushed and broken by My sentence because she is determined to follow idols.

12 I will destroy her as a moth does wool; I will sap away the strength of Judah like dry rot.

13 When Ephraim and Judah see how sick they are, Ephraim will turn to Assyria, to the great king there; but he can neither help nor cure.

*literally, "as those who move a boundary marker." See Deut. 19:14; 27:17.

14 I will tear Ephraim and Judah as a lion rips
apart its prey; I will carry them off and chase all
rescuers away.
15 I will abandon them and return to My home
until they admit their guilt and look to Me for
help again; for as soon as trouble comes, they will
search for Me and say:

CHAPTER 6

Come, let us return to the Lord; it is He who has
torn us—He will heal us. He has wounded—He will
bind us up.
2 In just a couple of days,* or three at the most,
He will set us on our feet again, to live in His kindness!
3 Oh that we might know the Lord! Let us press
on to know Him, and He will respond to us as surely
as the coming of dawn or the rain of early spring."
4 Oh Ephraim and Judah, what shall I do with
you? For your love vanishes like morning clouds,
and disappears like dew.
5 I sent My prophets to warn you of your doom;
I have slain you with the words of My mouth,
threatening you with death. Suddenly, without
warning, My judgment will strike you as surely as
day follows night.
6 I don't want your sacrifices—I want your love;
I don't want your offerings—I want you to know
Me.
7 But like Adam, you broke My covenant; you
refused My love.

*literally, "In two days."

8 Gilead is a city of sinners, tracked with foot-
prints of blood.

9 Her citizens are gangs of robbers, lying in am-
bush for their victims; packs of priests murder along
the road to Shechem and practice every kind of sin.

10 Yes, I have seen a horrible thing in Israel—
Ephraim chasing other gods, Israel utterly defiled.

11 Oh Judah, for you also there is a plentiful
harvest of punishment waiting—and I wanted so
much to bless you!

CHAPTER 7

I wanted to forgive Israel, but her sins were far too
great—no one can even live in Samaria without being a liar, thief and bandit!

2 Her people never seem to recognize that I am
watching them. Their sinful deeds give them away
on every side; I see them all.

3 The king is glad about their wickedness; the
princes laugh about their lies.

4 They are all adulterers; as a baker's oven is
constantly aflame—except while he kneads the
dough and waits for it to rise—so are these people
constantly aflame with lust.

5 On the king's birthday, the princes get him
drunk; he makes a fool of himself and drinks with
those who mock him.

6 Their hearts blaze like a furnace with intrigue.

Their plot smolders through the night, and in the morning it flames forth like raging fire.

7 They kill their kings one after another*, and none cries out to Me for help.

8 My people mingle with the heathen, picking up their evil ways; thus they become as good-for-nothing as a half-baked cake!

9 Worshiping foreign gods has sapped their strength, but they don't know it. Ephraim's hair is turning gray, and he doesn't even realize how weak and old he is.

10 His pride in other gods has openly condemned him; yet he doesn't return to his God, nor even try to find Him.

11 Ephraim is a silly, witless dove, calling to Egypt, flying to Assyria.

12 But as she flies, I throw My net over her and bring her down like a bird from the sky; I will punish her for all her evil ways.

13 Woe to My people for deserting Me; let them perish, for they have sinned against Me. I wanted to redeem them but their hard hearts would not accept the truth.

14 They lie there sleepless with anxiety, but won't ask My help. Instead, they worship heathen gods, asking them for crops and for prosperity.

15 I have helped them, and made them strong; yet now they turn against Me.

16 They look everywhere except to heaven, to the Most High God. They are like a crooked bow that always misses targets; their leaders will perish by

*Three Israelite kings were assassinated during Hosea's lifetime—Zechariah, Shallum and Pekahiah.

the sword of the enemy for their insolence to Me. And all Egypt will laugh at them.

CHAPTER 8

Sound the alarm! They are coming! Like a vulture, the enemy descends upon the people of God because they have broken My treaty and revolted against My laws.

2 Now Israel pleads with Me and says, "Help us, for You are our God!"

3 But it is too late! Israel has thrown away her chance disdainfully, and now her enemies will chase her.

4 She has appointed kings and princes, but not with My consent. They have cut themselves off from My help by worshiping the idols that they made from their silver and gold.

5 Oh Samaria, I reject this calf—this idol you have made. My fury burns against you. How long will it be before one honest man is found among you?

6 When will you admit this calf you worship was made by human hands! It is not God! Therefore, it must be smashed to bits.

7 They have sown the wind and they will reap the whirlwind. Their cornstalks stand there barren, withered, sickly, with no grain; if it has any, foreigners will eat it.

8 Israel is destroyed; she lies among the nations as a broken pot.

9 She is a lonely, wandering wild ass. The only
friends she has are those she hires; Assyria is one
of them.

10 But though she hires "friends" from many
lands, I will send her off to exile. Then for a while
at least she will be free of the burden of her
wonderful king!

11 Ephraim has built many altars, but they are
not to worship Me! They are altars of sin!

12 Even if I gave her ten thousand laws, she'd
say they weren't for her—that they applied to
someone far away.

13 Her people love the ritual of their sacrifice,
but to Me it is meaningless! I will call for an ac-
counting of their sins and punish them; they shall
return to Egypt.

14 Israel has built great palaces; Judah has con-
structed great defenses for her cities; but they have
forgotten their Maker. Therefore, I will send down
fire upon those palaces and burn those fortresses.

CHAPTER 9

Oh Israel, rejoice no more as others do, for you
have deserted your God and sacrificed to other gods
on every threshing floor.

2 Therefore your harvests will be small; your
grapes will blight upon the vine.

3 You may no longer stay here in this land of
God; you will be carried off to Egypt and Assyria,
and live there on scraps of food.

4 There, far from home, you are not allowed to

pour out wine for sacrifice to God. For no sacrifice that is offered there can please Him; it is polluted, just as food of mourners is; all who eat such sacrifices are defiled. They may eat this food to feed themselves, but may not offer it to God.

5 What then will you do on holy days, on days of feasting to the Lord,

6 When you are carried off to Assyria as slaves? Who will inherit your possessions left behind? Egypt will! She will gather your dead; Memphis will bury them. And thorns and thistles will grow up among the ruins.

7 The time of Israel's punishment has come; the day of recompense is almost here and soon Israel will know it all too well. "The prophets are crazy"; "The inspired men are mad." Yes, so they mock, for the nation is weighted with sin, and show only hatred for those who love God.

8 I appointed the prophets to guard My people, but the people have blocked them at every turn and publicly declared their hatred, even in the temple of the Lord.

9 The things My people do are as depraved as what they did in Gibeah* long ago. The Lord does not forget. He will surely punish them.

10 Oh Israel, how well I remember those first delightful days when I led you through the wilderness! How refreshing was your love! How satisfying, like the early figs of summer in their first season! But then you deserted Me for Baal-peor,† to give yourselves to other gods, and soon you were as foul as they.

*see Judges, chapter 9.
†Baal-peor, the god of Peor, a city of Moab. See Numbers, chapter 23.

11 The glory of Israel flies away like a bird, for your children will die at birth, or perish in the womb, or never even be conceived.

12 And if your children grow, I will take them from you; all are doomed. Yes, it will be a sad day when I turn away and leave you alone.

13 In my vision I have seen the sons of Israel doomed. The fathers are forced to lead their sons to slaughter.

14 Oh Lord, what shall I ask for Your people? I will ask for wombs that don't give birth; for breasts that cannot nourish.

15 All their wickedness began at Gilgal;* there I began to hate them. I will drive them from My land because of their idolatry. I will love them no more, for all their leaders are rebels.

16 Ephraim is doomed. The roots of Israel are dried up; she shall bear no more fruit. And if she gives birth, I will slay even her beloved child.

17 My God will destroy the people of Israel because they will not listen or obey. They will be wandering Jews, homeless among the nations.

CHAPTER 10

How prosperous Israel is—a luxuriant vine all filled with fruit! But the more wealth I give her, the more she pours it on the altars of her heathen gods; the richer the harvests I give her, the more beautiful the statues and idols she erects.

*Gilgal: the town where Baal-worship flourished (Hosea 4:15; 12:11), and where the monarchy, hated of God, was instituted (I Samuel 11:15).

2 The hearts of her people are false toward God. They are guilty and must be punished. God will break down their heathen altars and smash their idols.

3 Then they will say, "We deserted the Lord and He took away our king. But what's the difference? We don't need one anyway!"

4 They make promises they don't intend to keep. Therefore punishment will spring up among them like poisonous weeds in the furrows of the field.

5 The people of Samaria tremble lest their calf-god idols at Bethaven should be hurt; the priests and people, too, mourn over the departed honor of their shattered gods.

6 This idol—this calf-god thing—will be carted with them when they go as slaves to Assyria, a present to the great king there. Ephraim will be laughed at for trusting in this idol; Israel will be put to shame.

7 As for Samaria, her king shall disappear like a chip of wood upon an ocean wave.

8 And the idol altars of Aven at Bethel where Israel sinned will crumble. Thorns and thistles will grow up to surround them. And the people will cry to the mountains and hills to fall upon them and crush them.

9 Oh Israel, ever since that awful night in Gibeah,* there has been only sin, sin, sin! You have made no progress whatever. Was it not right that the men of Gibeah were wiped out?

10 I will come against you for your disobedience; I will gather the armies of the nations against you to punish you for your heaped-up sins.

*Judges, chapter 19, and 20.

11 Ephraim is accustomed to treading out the
grain—an easy job she loves; I have never put her
under a heavy yoke before; I have spared her
tender neck. But now I will harness her to the
plow and harrow. Her days of ease are gone.

12 Plant the good seeds of righteousness and you
will reap a crop of My love; plow the hard ground
of your hearts, for now is the time to seek the Lord,
that He may come and shower salvation upon you.

13 But you have cultivated wickedness and raised
a thriving crop of sins. You have earned the full
reward of trusting in a lie—believing that military
might and great armies can make a nation safe!

14 Therefore the terrors of war shall rise among
your people, and all your forts will fall, just as at
Betharbel, which Shalman* destroyed; even moth-
ers and children were dashed to death there.

15 That will be your fate, too, you people of
Israel, because of your great wickedness. In one
morning the king of Israel shall be destroyed.

CHAPTER 11

When Israel was a child I loved him as a son
and brought him out of Egypt.
2 But the more I called to him, the more he rebelled, sacrificing to Baal and burning incense to
idols.

3 I trained him from infancy; I taught him to

*Shalman: probably Salaman, King of Moab, who invaded Gilead around 740 B.C.

walk, I held him in My arms. But he doesn't know
or even care that it was I who raised him.
4 As a man would lead his favorite ox,* so I led
Israel with My ropes of love. I loosened his muzzle
so he could eat. I myself have stooped and fed him.
5 But My people shall return to Egypt and
Assyria because they won't return to Me.
6 War will swirl through their cities; their enemies will crash through their gates and trap them
in their own fortresses.
7 For My people are determined to desert Me.
And so I have sentenced them to slavery, and no
one shall set them free.
8 Oh, how can I give you up, My Ephraim?
How can I let you go? How can I forsake you like
Admah and Zeboim?† My heart cries out within
Me; how I long to help you!
9 No, I will not punish you as much as My fierce
anger tells Me to. This is the last time I will destroy Ephraim. For I am God and not man; I am
the Holy One living among you and I did not come
to destroy.
10 For the people shall walk after the Lord. I
shall roar as a lion (at their enemies)* and My
people shall return trembling from the west.
11 Like a flock of birds, they will come from
Egypt—like doves flying from Assyria. And I will
bring them home again; it is a promise from the
Lord.
12 Israel surrounds Me with lies and deceit; but
Judah still trusts in God and is faithful to the Holy
One.

*implied.
†Cities of the plain that perished with Sodom and Gomorrah (Deut. 29:23).

CHAPTER 12

Israel is chasing the wind, yes, shepherding a whirlwind—a dangerous game!* For she has given gifts
to Egypt and Assyria to get their help, and in return she gets their worthless promises.
2 But the Lord is bringing a lawsuit against
Judah,† too. Judah also will be justly punished
for his ways.
3 When he was born, he struggled with his
brother; when he became a man, he even fought
with God.
4 Yes, he wrestled with the Angel and prevailed.
He wept and pleaded for a blessing from Him. He
met God there at Bethel face to face. God spoke
to him—
5 The Lord, the God of Hosts; Jehovah is His
Name.
6 Oh, come back to God. Live by the principles
of love and justice, and always be expecting much
from Him, your God.
7 But no, My people are like crafty merchants
selling from dishonest scales—they love to cheat.
8 Ephraim boasts, "I am so rich! I have gotten
it all by myself!" But riches can't make up for sin.
9 I am the same Lord, the same God, who delivered you from slavery in Egypt, and I am the
One who will consign you to living in tents again,
as you do each year at the Tabernacle Feast.
10 I sent My prophets to warn you with many a
vision and many a parable and dream.
11 But the sins of Gilgal flourish just the same.

*implied.
†literally "Jacob."

Row on row of altars—like furrows in a field—are used for sacrifices to your idols. And Gilead, too, is full of fools* who worship idols.

12 Jacob fled to Syria and earned a wife by tending sheep.

13 Then the Lord led His people out of Egypt by a prophet, who guided and protected them.

14 But Ephraim has bitterly provoked the Lord. The Lord will sentence him to death as payment for his sins.

CHAPTER 13

It used to be when Israel spoke, the nations shook with fear, for he was a mighty prince; but he worshiped Baal and sealed his doom.

2 And now the people disobey more and more. They melt their silver to mold into idols, formed with skill by the hands of men. "Sacrifice to these!" they say—men kissing calves!

3 They shall disappear like morning mist; like dew that quickly dries away; like chaff blown by the wind; like a cloud of smoke.

4 I alone am God, your Lord, and have been ever since I brought you out from Egypt. You have no God but Me, for there is no other Savior.

5 I took care of you in the wilderness, in that dry and thirsty land.

*or, "vanity."

6 But when you had eaten and were satisfied, then you became proud and forgot Me.

7 So I will come upon you like a lion, or a leopard lurking along the road.

8 I will rip you to pieces like a bear whose cubs have been taken away; and like a lion I will devour you.

9 Oh Israel, if I destroy you, who can save you?

10 Where is your king? Why don't you call on him for help? Where are all the leaders of the land? You asked for them, now let them save you!

11 I gave you kings in My anger, and I took them away* in My wrath.

12 Ephraim's sins are harvested and stored away for punishment.

13 New birth is offered him, but he is like a child resisting in the womb—how stubborn! how foolish!

14 Shall I ransom him from Hell? Shall I redeem him from Death? Oh Death, bring forth your terrors for his tasting! Oh Grave, demonstrate your plagues! For I will not relent!

15 He was called the most fruitful of all his brothers, but the east wind—a wind of the Lord from the desert—will blow hard upon him and dry up his land. All his flowing springs and green oases will dry away, and he will die of thirst.

16 Samaria must bear her guilt, for she rebelled against her God. Her people will be killed by the invading army, her babies dashed to death against the ground, her pregnant women ripped open with a sword.

*Probably an allusion to the kings of Israel assassinated during her last tempestuous years: Zechariah, Shallum, Pekahiah.

CHAPTER 14

Oh Israel, return to the Lord, your God; for you
have been crushed by your sins.

2 Bring your petition. Come to the Lord and say,
"Oh Lord, take away our sins; be gracious to us
and receive us, and we will offer you the sacrifice
of praise.

3 "Assyria cannot save us, nor can our strength
in battle; never again will we call the idols we have
made 'our gods'; for in You alone, oh Lord, the
fatherless find mercy."

4 Then I will cure you of idolatry and faithless-
ness, and My love will know no bounds, for My
anger will be forever gone!

5 I will refresh Israel like the dew from heaven;
she will blossom as the lily and root deeply in the
soil like cedars in Lebanon.

6 Her branches will spread out as beautiful as
olive trees, fragrant as the forests of Lebanon.

7 Her people will return from exile far away and
rest beneath My shadow. They will be a watered
garden and blossom like grapes and be as fragrant
as the wines of Lebanon.

8 Oh Ephraim! Stay away from idols! I am living and strong! I look after you and care for you.
I am like an evergreen tree, yielding My fruit to
you throughout the year. My mercies never fail.

9 Whoever is wise, let him understand these
things. Whoever is intelligent, let him listen. For
the paths of the Lord are true and right, and good
men walk along them. But sinners trying it will fail.

Joel

CHAPTER 1

This message came from the Lord to Joel, son of Pethuel:

2 Listen, you aged men of Israel! Everyone, listen! In all your lifetime, yes, in all your history, have you ever heard of such a thing as I am going to tell you?

3 In years to come, tell your children about it; pass the awful story down from generation to generation:

4 For after the cutter-locusts finish eating your crops, the swarmer-locusts will take what's left! After them will come the hopper-locusts! And then the stripper-locusts, too!

5 Wake up and weep, you drunkards; for all the grapes are ruined and all your wine is gone!

6 A vast army of locusts* covers the land. It is a terrible army too numerous to count, with teeth as sharp as those of lions!

7 They have ruined My vines and stripped the bark from the fig trees, leaving trunks and branches white and bare.

8 Weep with sorrow, as a virgin weeps whose fiance' is dead.

9 Gone are the offerings of grain and wine to bring to the temple of the Lord; the priests are starving. Hear the crying of these ministers of God.

*literally, "a nation."

10 The fields are bare of crops. Sorrow and sadness are everywhere. The grain, the grapes, the
olive oil are gone.

11 Well may you farmers stand so shocked and
stricken; well may you vinedressers weep. Weep
for the wheat and the barley too, for they are gone.

12 The grapevines are dead; the fig trees are
dying; the pomegranates wither; the apples shrivel
on the trees; all joy has withered with them.

13 Oh priests, robe yourselves in sackcloth. Oh
ministers of my God, lie all night before the altar,
weeping. For there are no more offerings of grain
and wine for you.

14 Announce a fast; call a solemn meeting.
Gather the elders and all the people into the temple of the Lord your God, and weep before Him
there.

15 Alas, this terrible day of punishment* is on
the way. Destruction from the Almighty is almost
here!

16 Our food will disappear before our eyes; all
joy and gladness will be ended in the temple of our
God.

17 The seed rots in the ground; the barns and
granaries are empty; the grain has dried up in the
fields.

18 The cattle groan with hunger; the herds stand
perplexed for there is no pasture for them; the sheep
bleat in misery.

19 Lord, help us! For the heat has withered the
pastures and burned up all the trees.

20 Even the wild animals cry to You for help, for

*or, "the Day of the Lord."

there is no water for them. The creeks are dry and the pastures are scorched.

CHAPTER 2

Sound the alarm in Jerusalem! Let the blast of
the warning trumpet be heard upon My holy mountain! Let everyone tremble in fear, for the day of
the Lord's judgment approaches.
2 It is a day of darkness and gloom, of black
clouds and thick darkness. What a mighty army!
It covers the mountains like night! How great, how
powerful these "people" are! The likes of them
have not been seen before, and never will again
throughout the generations of the world!
3 Fire goes before them and follows them on
every side! Ahead of them the land lies fair as
Eden's Garden in all its beauty, but they destroy
it to the ground; not one thing escapes.
4 They look like tiny horses, and they run as
fast.
5 Look at them leaping along the tops of the
mountain! Listen to the noise they make, like the
rumbling of chariots, or the roar of fire sweeping
across a field; and like a mighty army moving into
battle.
6 Fear grips the waiting people; their faces grow
pale with fright.
7 These "soldiers" charge like infantry; they
scale the walls like picked and trained commandos.
Straight forward they march, never breaking ranks.
8 They never crowd each other. Each is right in
place. No weapon can stop them.

9 They swarm upon the city; they run upon the walls; they climb up into the houses, coming like thieves through the windows.

10 The earth quakes before them and the heavens tremble. The sun and moon are obscured and the stars are hid.

11 The Lord leads them with a shout. This is His mighty army and they follow His orders. The day of the judgment of the Lord is an awesome, terrible thing. Who can endure it?

12 That is why the Lord says, "Turn to Me now, while there is time. Give Me all your hearts. Come with fasting, weeping, mourning.

13 Let your remorse tear at your hearts and not your garments." Return to the Lord your God, for He is gracious and merciful. He is not easily angered; He is full of kindness, and anxious not to punish you.

14 Who knows? Perhaps even yet He will decide to let you alone and give you a blessing instead of His terrible curse. Perhaps He will give you so much that you can offer your grain and wine to the Lord as before!

15 Sound the trumpet in Zion! Call a fast and gather all the people together for a solemn meeting.

16 Bring everyone—the elders, the children, and even the babies. Call the bridegroom from his quarters and the bride from her privacy.

17 The priests, the ministers of God, will stand between the people and the altar, weeping; and they will pray, "Spare Your people, oh our God; don't let the heathen rule them, for they belong to You. Don't let them be disgraced by the taunts of the

heathen who say, 'Where is this God of theirs?
How weak and helpless He must be!' "
18 Then the Lord will pity His people and be
indignant for the honor of His land!
19 He will reply, "See, I am sending you much
corn and wine and oil, to fully satisfy your need.
No longer will I make you a laughingstock among
the nations.
20 I will remove these armies from the north and
send them far away; I will turn them back into the
parched wastelands where they will die; half shall
be driven into the Dead Sea and the rest into the
Mediterranean, and then their rotting stench will
rise upon the land. The Lord has done a mighty
miracle for you."

* * * *

21 Fear not, my people; be glad now and rejoice,
for He has done amazing things for you.
22 "Let the flocks and herds forget their hunger:
the pastures will turn green again. The trees will
bear their fruit: the fig trees and grapevines will
flourish once more.
23 Rejoice, oh people of Jerusalem, rejoice in the
Lord your God! For the rains He sends are tokens
of forgiveness. Once more the autumn rains will
come, as well as those of spring.
24 The threshing floors will pile high again with
wheat, and the presses overflow with olive oil and
wine.
25 And I will give you back the crops the locusts
ate!—My great destroying army that I sent against
you.
26 Once again you will have all the food you
want. Praise the Lord, who does these miracles for

you. And never again will My people experience disaster such as this.

27 And you will know that I am here among My people Israel, and that I alone am the Lord, your God. And My people shall never again be dealt a blow like this.

28 After I have poured out My rains again, I will pour out My Spirit upon all of you! Your sons and daughters will prophesy; your old men will dream dreams, and your young men see visions.

29 And I will pour out My Spirit even on your slaves, men and women alike,

30 And put strange symbols in the earth and sky —blood and fire and pillars of smoke.

31 The sun will be turned into darkness and the moon to blood before the great and terrible Day of the Lord shall come.

32 Everyone who calls upon the name of the Lord will be saved; even in Jerusalem some will escape, just as the Lord has promised; for He has chosen some to survive."

CHAPTER 3

At that time, when I restore the prosperity of Judah and Jerusalem," says the Lord,

2 "I will gather the armies of the world into the Valley Where Jehovah Judges* and punish them there for harming My people, for scattering My inheritance among the nations and dividing up My land.

*or, "Valley of Jehoshaphat."

3 They divided up My people as their slaves;
they traded a young lad for a prostitute, and a little
girl for wine enough to get drunk.

4 Tyre and Sidon, don't you try to interfere! Are
you trying to take revenge on Me, you cities of
Philistia? Beware, for I will strike back swiftly,
and return the harm to your own heads.

5 You have taken My silver and gold and all My
precious treasures and carried them off to your
heathen temples.

6 You have sold the people of Judah and Jerusalem to the Greeks, who took them far from their
own land.

7 But I will bring them back again from all these
places you have sold them to, and I will pay you
back for all that you have done.

8 I will sell your sons and daughters to the people of Judah and they will sell them to the Sabeans
far away. This is a promise from the Lord."

9 Announce this far and wide: Get ready for
war! Conscript your best soldiers; collect all your
armies.

10 Melt your plowshares into swords and beat
your pruning hooks into spears. Let the weak be
strong.

11 Gather together and come, all nations everywhere.

And now, oh Lord, bring down Your warriors!

12 Collect the nations; bring them to the Valley
of Jehoshaphat; for there I will sit to pronounce
judgment on them all.

13 Now let the sickle do its work; the harvest is

ripe and waiting. Tread the winepress, for it is full
to overflowing with the wickedness of these men.

14 Multitudes, multitudes waiting in the valley
for the verdict of their doom! For the Day of the
Lord is near, in the Valley of Judgment.

15 The sun and moon will be darkened and the
stars withdraw their light.

16 The Lord shouts from His temple in Jerusalem and the earth and sky begin to shake. But to
His people Israel, the Lord will be very gentle. He
is their Refuge and Strength.

17 "Then you shall know at last that I am the
Lord your God in Zion, My holy mountain. Jerusalem shall be Mine forever; the time will come
when no foreign armies will pass through her any
more.

18 Sweet wine will drip from the mountains, and
the hills shall flow with milk. Water will fill the dry
stream beds of Judah, and a fountain will burst
forth from the temple of the Lord to water Acacia
Valley.

19 Egypt will be destroyed, and Edom too, because of their violence against the Jews, for they
killed innocent people in those nations.

20 But Israel will prosper forever, and Jerusalem
will thrive as generations pass.

21 For I will avenge the blood of My people; I
will not clear their oppressors of guilt. For My
home is in Jerusalem* with My people."

*literally, "Zion."

Amos

CHAPTER 1

Amos was a herdsman living in the village of Tekoa. All day long he sat on the hillsides watching the sheep, keeping them from straying.

2 One day, in a vision, God told him some of the things that were going to happen to his nation, Israel. This vision came to him at the time Uzziah was king of Judah, and while Jeroboam, (son of Joash), was king of Israel—two years before the earthquake.

This is his report of what he saw and heard: The Lord roared—like a ferocious lion from his lair—from His temple on Mount Zion. And suddenly the lush pastures of Mount Carmel withered and dried, and all the shepherds mourned.

* * * *

3 The Lord says, "The people of Damascus have sinned again and again, and I will not forget it. I will not leave her unpunished any more. For they have threshed My people in Gilead like grain is threshed with iron rods.

4 So I will set fire to King Hazael's palace, destroying the strong fortress of Benhadad.

5 I will snap the bars that locked the gates of Damascus, and kill her people as far away as the

plain of Aven; and the people of Syria shall return to Kir* as slaves." The Lord has spoken.

* * * *

6 The Lord says, "Gaza has sinned again and again, and I will not forget it. I will not leave her unpunished any more. For she sent My people into exile, selling them as slaves in Edom.

7 So I will set fire to the walls of Gaza, and all her forts shall be destroyed.

8 I will kill the people of Ashdod, and destroy Ekron and the king of Ashkelon: all Philistines left will perish." The Lord has spoken.

* * * *

9 The Lord says, "The people of Tyre have sinned again and again and I will not forget it. I will not leave them unpunished any more. For they broke their treaty with their brother, Israel; they attacked and conquered him, and led him into slavery to Edom.

10 So I will set fire to the walls of Tyre, and it will burn down all his forts and palaces."

* * * *

11 The Lord says, "Edom has sinned again and again, and I will not forget it. I will not leave him unpunished any more. For he chased his brother, Israel, with the sword; he was pitiless in unrelenting anger.

12 So I will set fire to Teman, and it will burn down all the forts of Bozrah."†

*Decreeing that the Syrians should go back to Kir as slaves was like saying to the Israelites that they must go back to Egypt as slaves, for the Syrians had made their exodus from Kir and now were free. (See 9:7).

†Teman was in the north of Edom, and Bozrah in the south. The entire country would be devastated.

* * * *

13 The Lord says, "The people of Ammon have
sinned again and again, and I will not forget it. I
will not leave them unpunished any more. For in
their wars in Gilead to enlarge their borders, they
committed cruel crimes, ripping open pregnant
women with their swords.
14 So I will set fire to the walls of Rabah, and it
will burn down their forts and palaces; there will be
wild shouts of battle like a whirlwind in a mighty
storm.
15 And their king and his princes will go into exile
together." The Lord has spoken.

CHAPTER 2

The Lord says, "The people of Moab have sinned
again and again, and I will not forget it. I will not
leave them unpunished any more. For they dese-
crated the tombs of the kings of Edom, with no
respect for the dead.
2 Now in return I will send fire upon Moab, and
it will destroy all the palaces in Kirioth. Moab shall
go down in tumult as the warriors shout and trumpets blare.
3 And I will destroy their king and slay all the
leaders under him." The Lord has spoken.

* * * *

4 The Lord says, "The people of Judah have
sinned again and again, and I will not forget it. I
will not leave them unpunished any more. For they
have rejected the laws of God, refusing to obey
Him. They have hardened their hearts and sinned
as their fathers did.

5 So I will destroy Judah with fire, and burn down all Jerusalem's palaces and forts."

* * * *

6 The Lord says, "The people of Israel have sinned again and again, and I will not forget it. I will not leave them unpunished any more. For they have perverted justice by accepting bribes, and sold into slavery the poor who can't repay their debts; they trade them for a pair of shoes.

7 They trample the poor in the dust and kick aside the meek. And a man and his father defile the same temple-girl, corrupting My holy Name.

8 At their religious feasts they lounge in clothing stolen from their debtors,* and in My own temple they offer sacrifices of wine they purchased with stolen money.

9 Yet think of all I did for them! I cleared the land of the Amorites before them—the Amorites, as tall as cedar trees, and strong as oaks! But I lopped off their fruit and cut their roots.

10 And I brought you out from Egypt and led you through the desert forty years, to possess the land of the Amorites.

11 And I chose your sons to be Nazirites† and prophets—can you deny this, Israel?" asks the Lord.

12 "But you caused the Nazirites to sin by urging them to drink your wine, and you silenced My prophets, telling them, 'Shut up!'

*Under Mosaic Law, it was illegal to keep pledged clothing of debtors overnight. See Exodus 22:26.
†See Numbers, chapter 6.

13 Therefore I will make you groan as a wagon groans that is loaded with sheaves.

14 Your swiftest warriors will stumble in flight. The strong will all be weak, and the great ones can no longer save themselves.

15 The archer's aim will fail, the swiftest runners won't be fast enough to flee, and even the best of horsemen can't outrun the danger then.

16 The most courageous of your mighty men will drop their weapons and run for their lives that day." The Lord God has spoken.

CHAPTER 3

Listen! This is your doom! It is spoken by the Lord against both Israel and Judah—against the entire family I brought from Egypt:

2 "Of all the peoples of the earth, I have chosen you alone. That is why I must punish you the more for all your sins.

3 For how can we walk together with your sins between us?

4 Would I be roaring as a lion unless I had a reason? The fact is, I am getting ready to destroy you. Even a young lion, when it growls, shows it is ready for its food.

5 A trap doesn't snap shut unless it is stepped on; your punishment is well-deserved.

6 The alarm has sounded—listen and fear! For I, the Lord, am sending disaster into your land.

7 But always, first of all, I warn you through My
prophets. This I now have done."

8 The Lion has roared—tremble in fear. The
Lord God has sounded your doom—I dare not refuse to proclaim it.

* * * *

9 Call together the Assyrian and Egyptian leaders, saying, "Take your seats now on the mountains
of Samaria to witness the scandalous spectacle of
all Israel's crimes."

10 "My people have forgotten what it means to
do right," says the Lord. "Their beautiful homes
are full of the loot from their thefts and banditry.

11 Therefore," the Lord God says, "an enemy is
coming! He is surrounding them and will shatter
their forts and plunder those beautiful homes."

12 The Lord says, "A shepherd tried to rescue his
sheep from a lion, but it was too late: he snatched
from the lion's mouth two legs and a piece of ear.
So it will be when the Israelites in Samaria are
finally rescued—all they will have left is half a
chair and a tattered pillow.

13 Listen to this announcement, and publish it
throughout all Israel," says the Lord, the God of
Hosts:

14 "On the same day that I punish Israel for her
sins, I will also destroy the idol altars at Bethel.
The horns of the altar will be cut off and fall to the
ground.

15 And I will destroy the beautiful homes of the
wealthy—their winter mansions and their summer
houses, too—and demolish their ivory palaces."

CHAPTER 4

Listen to Me, you "fat cows" of Bashan living in Samaria—you women who encourage your husbands to rob the poor and crush the needy—you who never have enough to drink!

2 The Lord God has sworn by His holiness that the time will come when He will put hooks in your noses and lead you away like the cattle you are; they will drag the last of you away with fishhooks!

3 You will be hauled from your beautiful homes and tossed out through the nearest breach in the wall. The Lord has said it.

4 Go ahead and sacrifice to idols at Bethel and Gilgal. Keep disobeying—your sins are mounting up. Sacrifice each morning and bring your tithes twice a week!

5 Go through all your proper forms and give extra offerings. How you pride yourselves and crow about it everywhere!

6 "I sent you hunger," says the Lord, "but it did no good; you still would not return to Me.

7 I ruined your crops by holding back the rain three months before the harvest. I sent rain on one city, but not another. While rain fell on one field, another was dry and withered.

8 People from two or three cities would make their weary journey for a drink of water to a city that had rain, but there wasn't ever enough. Yet you wouldn't return to Me," says the Lord.

9 "I sent blight and mildew on your farms and

your vineyards; the locusts ate your figs and olive trees. And still you wouldn't return to Me," says the Lord.

10 "I sent you plagues like those of Egypt long ago. I killed your lads in war and drove away your horses. The stench of death was terrible to smell. And yet you refused to come.

11 I destroyed some of your cities, as I did Sodom and Gomorrah; those left are like half-burned fire-brands snatched away from fire. And still you won't return to Me," says the Lord.

12 "Therefore I will bring upon you all these further evils I have spoken of. Prepare to meet your God in judgment, Israel.

13 For you are dealing with the One who formed the mountains and made the winds, and knows your every thought; He turns the morning to darkness and crushes down the mountains underneath His feet: Jehovah, the Lord, the God of Hosts, is His Name."

CHAPTER 5

Sadly I sing this song of grief for you, oh Israel:

2 "Beautiful Israel lies broken and crushed upon the ground and cannot rise. No one will help her. She is left alone to die."

3 For the Lord God says, "The city that sends a thousand men to battle, a hundred will return. The city that sends a hundred, only ten will come back alive."

4 The Lord says to the people of Israel, "Seek Me—and live.

5 Don't seek the idols of Bethel, Gilgal, or Beer-sheba; for the people of Gilgal will be carried off to exile, and those of Bethel shall surely come to grief."

6 Seek the Lord and live, or else He will sweep like fire through Israel and consume her, and none of the idols in Bethel can put it out.

7 Oh evil men, you make "justice" a bitter pill for the poor and oppressed. "Righteousness" and "fair play" are meaningless fictions to you!

8 Seek Him who created the Seven Stars and the constellation Orion; who turns darkness into morning, and day into night; who calls forth the water from the ocean and pours it out as rain upon the land. The Lord, Jehovah, is His name.

9 With blinding speed and violence He brings destruction on the strong, breaking all defenses.

10 How you hate honest judges! How you despise people who tell the truth!

11 You trample the poor and steal their smallest crumb by all your taxes, fines, and usury; therefore you will never live in the beautiful stone houses you are building, nor drink the wine from the lush vineyards you are planting.

12 For many and great are your sins. I know them all so well. You are the enemies of everything good; you take bribes; you refuse justice to the poor.

13 Therefore those who are wise will not try to
interfere with the Lord in the dread Day of your
punishment.
14 Be good, flee evil—and live! Then the Lord
God of Hosts will truly be your Helper, as you have
claimed He is.
15 Hate evil and love the good; remodel your
courts into true halls of justice. Perhaps even yet
the Lord God of hosts will have mercy on His people
who remain.
16 Therefore the Lord God of Hosts says this:
"There will be crying in all the streets and every
road. Call for the farmers to weep with you, too;
call for professional mourners to wail and lament.
17 There will be sorrow and crying in every vine-
yard. For I will pass through and destroy.
18 You say, 'If only the Day of the Lord were
here, for then God would deliver us from all our
foes.' But you have no idea what you ask. For that
Day will *not* be light and prosperity, but darkness
and doom! How terrible the darkness will be for
you; not a ray of joy or hope will shine.
19 In that Day you will be as a man who is
chased by a lion—and met by a bear; or a man in
a dark room who leans against a wall—and puts his
hand on a snake.
20 Yes, that will be a dark and hopeless day for
you.
21 I hate your show and pretense—your hypoc-
risy of 'honoring' Me with your religious feasts and
solemn assemblies.
22 I will not accept your burnt-offerings and
thank-offerings. I will not look at your offerings of
peace.

23 Away with your hymns of praise—they are mere noise to My ears. I will not listen to your music, no matter how lovely it is.

24 I want to see a mighty flood of justice—a torrent of doing good.

25, 26, 27 You sacrificed to Me for forty years while you were in the desert, Israel—but always your real interest has been in your heathen gods—in Sakkuth your king, and in Kaiwan, your god of the stars, and in all the images of them you made. So I will send them into captivity with you far to the east of Damascus," says the Lord, the God of Hosts.

CHAPTER 6

Woe to those lounging in luxury at Jerusalem and Samaria, so famous and popular among the people of Israel.

2 Go over to Calneh and see what happened there; then go to great Hamath and down to Gath in the Philistines' land. Once they were better and greater than you, but look at them now.

3 You push away all thought of punishment awaiting you, but by your deeds you bring the Day of Judgment near.

4 You lie on ivory beds surrounded with luxury, eating the meat of the tenderest lambs and the choicest calves.

5 You sing idle songs to the sound of the harp, and fancy yourselves to be as great musicians as King David was.

6 You drink wine by the bucketful and perfume yourselves with sweet ointments, caring nothing at all that your brothers need your help.

7 Therefore you will be the first to be taken as slaves; suddenly your revelry will end.

8 Jehovah, the Lord God of Hosts, has sworn by His own Name, "I despise the pride and false glory of Israel, and hate their beautiful homes. I will turn over this city and everything in it to her enemies."

9 If there are as few as ten of them left, and even one house, they too will perish.

10 A man's uncle will be the only one left to bury him, and when he goes in to carry his body from the house, he will ask the only one still alive inside, "Are any others left?" And the answer will be, "No," and he will add, "Shhh . . . don't mention the Name of the Lord—He might hear you."

11 For the Lord commanded this: That homes both great and small should be smashed to pieces.

12 Can horses run on rocks? Can oxen plow the sea? Stupid even to ask, but no more stupid than what you do when you make a mockery of justice, and corrupt and sour all that should be good and right.

13 And just as stupid is your rejoicing in how great you are, when you are less than nothing! And priding yourselves on your own tiny power!

14 "Oh Israel, I will bring against you a nation that will bitterly oppress you from your northern boundary to your southern tip, all the way from Hamath to the brook of Arabah," says the Lord, the God of Hosts.

CHAPTER 7

This is what the Lord God showed me in a vision: He was preparing a vast swarm of locusts to destroy all the main crop that sprang up after the first mowing, which went as taxes to the king.

2 They ate everything in sight. Then I said, "Oh Lord God, please forgive Your people! Don't send them this plague! If You turn against Israel, what hope is there? For Israel is so small!"

3 So the Lord relented, and did not fulfill the vision. "I won't do it," He told me.

4 Then the Lord God showed me a great fire He had prepared to punish them; it had burned up the waters and was devouring the entire land.

5 Then I said, "Oh Lord God, please don't do it. If you turn against them, what hope is there? For Israel is so small!"

6 Then the Lord turned from this plan too, and said, "I won't do that either."

7 Then He showed me this: the Lord was standing beside a wall built with a plumbline, checking it with a plumbline to see if it was straight.

8 And the Lord said to me, "Amos, what do you see?" I answered, "A plumbline." And He replied, "I will test My people with a plumbline. I will no longer turn away from punishing.

9 The idol altars and temples of Israel will be destroyed; and I will destroy the dynasty of King Jeroboam by the sword."

10 But when Amaziah, the priest of Bethel, heard

what Amos was saying, he rushed a message to
Jeroboam, the king: "Amos is a traitor to our nation
and is plotting your death. This is intolerable. It
will lead to rebellion all across the land.

11 He says you will be killed, and Israel will be
sent far away into exile and slavery."

12 Then Amaziah sent orders to Amos, "Get out
of here, you prophet, you! Flee to the land of Judah
and do your prophesying there!

13 Don't bother us here with your visions; not
here in the capital, where the king's chapel is!"

14 But Amos replied, "I am not really one of the
prophets. I do not come from a family of prophets.
I am just a herdsman and fruit picker.

15 But the Lord took me from caring for the
flocks and told me, 'Go and prophesy to My people
Israel.'

16 Now therefore listen to this message to you
from the Lord. You say, 'Don't prophesy against
Israel.'

17 The Lord's reply is this: 'Because of your in-
terference, your wife will become a prostitute in this
city, and your sons and daughters will be killed and
your land divided up. You yourself will die in a
heathen land, and the people of Israel will certainly
become slaves in exile, far from their land.' "

CHAPTER 8

Then the Lord God showed me, in a vision, a
basket full of ripe fruit.

2 "What do you see, Amos?" He asked.

I replied, "A basket full of ripe fruit."

Then the Lord said, "This fruit represents My people Israel—ripe for punishment. I will not defer their punishment again.

3 The riotous sound of singing in the temple will turn to weeping then. Dead bodies will be scattered everywhere. They will be carried out of the city in silence." The Lord has spoken.

4 Listen, you merchants who rob the poor, trampling on the needy;

5 You who long for the Sabbath to end and the religious holidays to be over, so you can get out and start cheating again—using your weighted scales and under-sized measures;

6 You who make slaves of the poor, buying them for their debt of a piece of silver or a pair of shoes, or selling them your moldy wheat—

7 The Lord, the Pride of Israel, has sworn: "I won't forget your deeds!

8 The land will tremble as it awaits its doom, and everyone will mourn. It will rise up like the River Nile at floodtime, toss about, and sink again.

9 At that time I will make the sun go down at noon and darken the earth in the daytime.

10 And I will turn your parties into times of mourning, and your songs of joy will be turned to cries of despair. You will wear funeral clothes and shave your heads as signs of sorrow, as if your only son had died; bitter, bitter will be that Day."

11 "The time is surely coming," says the Lord God, "when I will send a famine on the land—not a famine of bread or water, but of hearing the words of the Lord.

12 Men will wander everywhere from sea to sea, seeking the Word of the Lord, searching, running here and going there, but will not find it.

13 Beautiful girls and fine young men alike will grow faint and weary, thirsting for the Word of God.

14 And those who worship the idols of Samaria, Dan, and Beersheba shall fall and never rise again."

CHAPTER 9

I saw the Lord standing beside the altar saying, "Smash the tops of the pillars and shake the temple until the pillars crumble and the roof crashes down upon the people below. Though they run, they will not escape; they all will be killed.

2 Though they dig down to Sheol, I will reach down and pull them up; though they climb into the heavens, I will bring them down.

3 Though they hide among the rocks at the top of Carmel, I will search them out and capture them. Though they hide at the bottom of the ocean, I will send the sea-serpent after them to bite and destroy them.

4 Though they volunteer for exile, I will command the sword to kill them there. I will see to it that they receive evil and not good."

5 The Lord God of Hosts touches the land and it

melts; and all its people mourn. It rises like the River Nile in Egypt, and then sinks again.

6 The upper stories of His home are in the heavens, the first floor on the earth. He calls for the vapor to rise from the ocean and pours it down as rain upon the ground. Jehovah, the Lord, is His Name.

7 "Oh people of Israel, are you any more to Me than the Ethiopians are? Have not I, who brought you out of Egypt, done as much for other people, too? I brought the Philistines from Caphtor and the Syrians out of Kir.

8 The eyes of the Lord God are watching Israel, that sinful nation, and I will root her up and scatter her across the world. Yet I have promised that this rooting out will not be permanent.

9 For I have commanded that Israel be sifted by the other nations as grain is sifted in a sieve, yet not one true kernel will be lost.

10 But all these sinners who say, 'God will not touch us,' will die by the sword.

11 Then, at that time, I will rebuild the City of David, which is now lying in ruins, and return it to its former glory,

12 And Israel will possess what is left of Edom, and of all the nations that belong to me." For so the Lord, who plans it all, has said.

13 "The time will come when there will be such abundance of crops, that the harvest time will scarcely end before the farmer starts again to sow another crop, and the terraces of grapes upon the hills of Israel will drip sweet wine!

14 I will restore the fortunes of My people Israel,
and they shall rebuild their ruined cities, and live
in them again; and they shall plant vineyards and
gardens and eat their crops and drink their wine.

15 I will firmly plant them there upon the land
that I have given them; they shall not be pulled up
again," says the Lord your God.

Obadiah

*In a vision, the Lord God showed Obadiah the future of the land of Edom.**

"A report has come from the Lord," he said, "that God has sent an ambassador to the nations with this message: 'Attention! You are to send your armies against Edom and destroy her!' "

* * * *

2 I will cut you down to size among the nations, Edom, making you small and despised.

3 You are proud because you live in those high, inaccessible cliffs. "Who can ever reach us way up here!" you boast. Don't fool yourselves!

4 Though you soar as high as eagles, and build your nest among the stars, I will bring you plummeting down, says the Lord.

5 Far better it would be for you if thieves had come at night to plunder you—for they would not take everything! or if your vineyards were robbed of all their fruit—for at least the gleanings would be left!

6 Every nook and cranny will be searched and robbed, and every treasure found and taken.

7 All your allies will turn against you and help to push you out of your land. They will promise peace while plotting your destruction. Your trusted friends will set traps for you and all your counterstrategy will fail.

*A nation southeast of Israel, including Petra, the city hewn from rocks; her southern boundary was on the Gulf of Aqaba.

8 In that day not one wise man* will be left in all of Edom! says the Lord. For I will fill the wise men of Edom with stupidity.

9 The mightiest soldiers of Teman will be confused, and helpless to prevent the slaughter.

10 And why? Because of what you did to your brother Israel. Now your sins will be exposed for all to see; ashamed and defenseless, you will be cut off forever.

11 For you deserted Israel in his time of need. You stood aloof, refusing to lift a finger to help him when invaders carried off his wealth and divided Jerusalem among them by lot; you were as one of his enemies.

12 You should not have done it. You should not have gloated when they took him far away to foreign lands; you should not have rejoiced in the day of his misfortune; you should not have mocked in his time of need.

13 You yourselves went into the land of Israel in the day of his calamity and looted him. You made yourselves rich at his expense.

14 You stood at the crossroads and killed those trying to escape; you captured the survivors and returned them to their enemies in that terrible time of his distress.

15 The Lord's vengeance will soon fall upon all heathen nations. As you have done to Israel, so will it be done to you. Your acts will boomerang upon your heads.

*Edom was noted for her wise men; Eliphaz, the wisest of Job's three friends, was from Teman, 5 miles east of Petra, in Edom.

16 You drank My cup of punishment upon My holy mountain, and the nations round about will drink it, too; yes, drink and stagger back and disappear from history, no longer nations any more.

17 But Jerusalem will become a refuge, a way of escape. Israel will reoccupy the land.

18 Israel will be a fire that sets the dry fields of Edom aflame. There will be no survivors, for the Lord has spoken.

19 Then My people who live in the Negeb shall occupy the hill country of Edom; those living in Judean lowlands shall possess the Philistine plains, and repossess the fields of Ephraim and Samaria. And the people of Benjamin shall possess Gilead.

20 The Israeli exiles shall return and occupy the Phoenician coastal strip as far north as Zarephath. Those exiled in Asia Minor shall return to their homeland and conquer the Negeb's outlying villages.

21 For deliverers will come to Jerusalem and rule all Edom. And the Lord shall be King!

Jonah

CHAPTER 1

The Lord sent this message to Jonah, the son of Amittai:

2 "Go to the great city of Nineveh, and give them this announcement from the Lord: 'I am going to destroy you; for your wickedness rises before Me; it smells to highest heaven.' "

3 But Jonah was afraid to go and ran away from the Lord. He went down to the seacoast, to the port of Joppa, where he found a ship leaving for Tarshish. He bought a ticket, went on board, and climbed down into the dark hole of the ship to hide there from the Lord.

4 But as the ship was sailing along, suddenly the Lord flung a terrific wind over the sea, causing a great storm that threatened to send them to the bottom.

5 Fearing for their lives, the desperate sailors shouted to their gods for help and threw the cargo overboard to lighten the ship. And all this time Jonah was sound asleep down in the hold.

6 So the captain went down after him. "What do you mean," he roared, "sleeping at a time like this? Get up and cry to your god, and see if he will have mercy on us and save us!"

7 Then the crew decided to draw straws to see which of them had offended the gods and caused this terrible storm; and Jonah drew the short one.

8 "What have you done," they asked, "to bring this awful storm upon us? Who are you? What is your work? What country are you from? What is your nationality?"

9,10 And he said, "I am a Jew;* I worship Jehovah, the God of heaven, who made the earth and sea." Then he told them he was running away from the Lord. The men were terribly frightened when they heard this. "Oh, why did you do it?" they shouted;

11 "And what should we do to you to stop the storm?" For it was getting worse and worse.

12 "Throw me out into the sea," he said, "and it will become calm again. For I know this terrible storm has come because of me."

13 They tried harder to row the boat ashore, but couldn't make it. The storm was too fierce to fight against.

14 Then they shouted out a prayer to Jehovah, Jonah's God. "Oh Jehovah," they pleaded, "don't make us die for this man's sin; and don't hold us responsible for his death, for it is not our fault—You have sent this storm upon him for Your own good reasons."

15 Then they picked up Jonah and threw him overboard into the raging sea—and the storm stopped!

16 The men stood there in awe before Jehovah, and sacrificed to Him and vowed to serve Him.

17 Now the Lord had arranged for a huge fish to swallow Jonah. And Jonah was inside the fish three days and three nights.

*literally, "a Hebrew."

CHAPTER 2

Then Jonah prayed to the Lord his God from inside the fish:

2 "In my great trouble I cried to the Lord and He answered me; from the depths of death I called, and Lord, You heard me!

3 You threw me into the ocean depths; I sank down into the floods of waters and was covered by Your wild and stormy waves.

4 Then I said, 'Oh Lord, You have rejected me and cast me away. How shall I ever again see Your holy temple?'

5 I sank beneath the waves, and death was very near. The waters closed above me; the seaweed wrapped itself around my head.

6 I went down to the bottoms of the mountains that rise from off the ocean floor. I was locked out of life and imprisoned in the land of death. But, oh Lord my God, You have snatched me from the yawning jaws of death!

7 When I had lost all hope, I turned my thoughts once more to the Lord. And my earnest prayer went to You in Your holy temple.

8 (Those who worship false gods have turned their backs on all the mercies waiting for them from the Lord!)

9 I will never worship anyone but You! For how can I thank You enough for all You have done? I

will surely fulfill my promises. For my deliverance
comes from the Lord alone."
10 And the Lord ordered the fish to spit up Jonah
on the beach, and it did.

CHAPTER 3

Then the Lord spoke to Jonah again: "Go to that
great city, Nineveh," He said, "and warn them of
their doom, as I told you to before!"
3 So Jonah obeyed, and went to Nineveh. Now
Nineveh was a very large city, with extensive suburbs—so large that it would take three days to walk
around it.*
4, 5 But the very first day when Jonah entered
the city and began to preach, the people repented.
Jonah shouted to the crowds that gathered around
him, "Forty days from now Nineveh will be destroyed!" And they believed him and declared a
fast; from the king on down everyone put on sackcloth—the rough, coarse garments worn at times of
mourning.†
6 For when the king of Nineveh heard what
Jonah was saying, he stepped down from his
throne and laid aside his royal robes and put on
sackcloth and sat in ashes.
7 And the king and his nobles sent this message
throughout the city: "Let no one, not even the
animals, eat anything at all, nor even drink any
water.
8 Everyone must wear sackcloth and cry mightily

*The Hebrew text makes no distinction between the city proper—the walls of which were only about 8 miles in circumference accommodating a population of about 175,000 persons—and the administrative district of Nineveh which was about 30-60 miles across.

†implied.

to God; and let everyone turn from his evil ways, from his violence and robbing.

9 Who can tell? Perhaps even yet God will decide to let us live, and will hold back His fierce anger from destroying us."

10 And when God saw that they had put a stop to their evil ways, He abandoned His plan to destroy them, and didn't carry it through.

CHAPTER 4

This change of plans made Jonah very angry.

2 He complained to the Lord about it: "This is exactly what I thought You'd do, Lord, when I was there in my own country and You first told me to come here. That's why I ran away to Tarshish. For I knew You were a gracious God, merciful, slow to get angry, and full of kindness; I knew how easily You could cancel Your plans for destroying these people.

3 Please kill me, Lord; I'd rather be dead than alive (when nothing that I told them happens*)."

4 Then the Lord said, "Is it right to be *angry* about *this?*"

5 So Jonah went out and sat sulking* on the east side of the city, and he made a leafy shelter to shade him as he waited there to see if anything would happen to the city.

6 And when the leaves of the shelter withered in the heat, the Lord arranged for a vine to grow up

*implied.

quickly and spread its broad leaves over Jonah's head to shade him. This made him comfortable and very grateful.

7 But God also prepared a worm! The next morning the worm ate through the stem of the plant, so that it withered away and died.

8 Then, when the sun was hot, God ordered a scorching east wind to blow on Jonah, and the sun beat down upon his head until he grew faint and wished to die. For he said, "Death is better than this!"

9 And God said to Jonah, "Is it right for you to be angry because the plant died?"

"Yes," Jonah said, "it is; it is right for me to be angry enough to die!"

10 Then the Lord said, "You feel sorry for yourself when your shelter is destroyed, though you did no work to put it there, and it is, at best, short-lived.

11 And why shouldn't I feel sorry for a great city like Nineveh with its 120,000 people in utter spiritual darkness, and all its cattle?"

Micah

CHAPTER 1

These are messages from the Lord to Micah, who lived in the town of Moresheth during the reigns of King Jotham, King Ahaz and King Hezekiah, all kings of Judah. The messages were addressed to both Samaria and Judah, and came to Micah in the form of visions.

2 Attention! Let all the peoples of the world listen. For the Lord in His holy temple has made accusations against you!

3 Look! He is coming! He leaves His throne in heaven and comes to earth, walking on the mountain tops.

4 They melt beneath His feet, and flow into the valleys like wax in fire, like water pouring down a hill.

5 And why is this happening?
Because of the sins of Israel and Judah.
What sins?
The idolatry and oppression centering in the capital cities, Samaria and Jerusalem!

6 Therefore the entire city of Samaria will crumble into a heap of rubble, and become an open field, her streets plowed up for planting grapes! The Lord will tear down her wall and her forts exposing their foundations, and pour their stones into the valleys below.

7 All her carved images will be smashed to pieces;

her ornate idol temples, built with the gifts of worshipers, will all be burned.*

* * * *

8 I will wail and lament, howling as a jackal, mournful as an ostrich crying across the desert sands at night. I will walk naked and barefoot in sorrow and shame;

9 For my people's wound is far too deep to heal. The Lord stands ready at Jerusalem's gates to punish her.

10 Woe to the city of Gath. Weep, men of Bakah. In Beth-le-Aphrah roll in the dust in your anguish and shame.

11 There go the people of Shaphir,† led away as slaves—stripped, naked and ashamed. The people of Zaanan† dare not show themselves outside their walls. The foundations of Beth-ezel† are swept away—the very ground on which it stood.

12 The people of Maroth vainly hope for better days, but only bitterness awaits them as the Lord stands poised against Jerusalem.

13 Quick! Use your swiftest chariots and flee, oh people of Lachish, for you were the first of the cities of Judah to follow Israel in her sin of idol worship. Then all the cities of the south began to follow your example.

14 Write off Moresheth‡ of Gath; there is no hope

*literally, "they shall return to the hire of an harlot."

†In the Hebrew, there is frequent word play in verses 10-14. Micah bitterly declaims each town, demonstrating by the use of puns their failures. *Shaphir* sounds like the Hebrew word for "beauty," here contrasted with their shame; *Zaanan* sounds like a verb meaning "to go forth," here contrasted with the fear of its inhabitants to venture outside; *Beth-ezel* sounds like a word for "foundation," which has been taken away from them.

‡Micah's home town. See verse 1 of chapter 1.

of saving her. The town of Achzib has deceived the kings of Israel, for she promised help she cannot give.

15 You people of Mareshah will be a prize to your enemies. They will penetrate to Adullum, the "Pride of Israel."

16 Weep, weep for your little ones. For they are snatched away and you will never see them again. They have gone as slaves to distant lands. Shave your heads in sorrow.

CHAPTER 2

Woe to you who lie awake at night, plotting wickedness; you rise at dawn to carry out your schemes; because you can, you do.

2 You want a certain piece of land, or someone else's house (though it is all he has); you take it by fraud and threats and violence.

* * * *

3 But the Lord God says, I will reward your evil with evil; nothing can stop Me; never again will you be proud and haughty after I am through with you.

4 Then your enemies will taunt you and mock your dirge of despair: "We are finished, ruined. God has confiscated our land and sent us far away, and given what is ours to others."

5 Others will set your boundaries then. "The People of the Lord" will live where they are sent.

6 "Don't say such things," the people say.

"Don't harp on things like that. It's disgraceful, that sort of talk. Such evils surely will not come our way."

7 Is that the right reply for you to make, oh House of Jacob? Do you think the Spirit of the Lord likes to talk to you so roughly? No! His threats are for your good, to get you on the path again.

8 Yet to this very hour My people rise against Me. For you steal the shirts right off the backs of those who trusted you, who walk in peace.

9 You have driven out the widows from their homes, and stripped their children of every God-given right.

10 Up! Begone! This is no more your land and home; for you have filled it with sin and it will vomit you out.

11 "I'll preach to you the joys of wine and drink"—that is the kind of drunken, lying prophet that you like!

* * * *

12 The time will come, oh Israel, when I will gather you—all that are left—and bring you together again like sheep in a fold, like a flock in a pasture—a noisy, happy crowd.

13 The Messiah* will lead you out of exile and bring you through the gates of your cities of captivity, back to your own land. Your King will go before you—the Lord leads on.

*"He who opens the breach."

* * * *

CHAPTER 3

Listen, you leaders of Israel—you are supposed to know right from wrong,

2 Yet you are the very ones who hate good and love evil; you skin My people and strip them to the bone.

3 You devour them, flog them, break their bones, and chop them up like meat for the cooking pot—

4 And then you plead with the Lord for His help in times of trouble! Do you really expect Him to listen? He will look the other way!

5 You false prophets! You who lead His people astray! You who cry "Peace" to those who give you food, and threaten those who will not pay! This is God's message to you:

6 The night will close about you and cut off all your visions; darkness will cover you, with never a word from God. The sun will go down upon you and your day will end.

7 Then at last you will cover your faces in shame, and admit that your messages were not from God.

8 But as for me, I am filled with power, with the Spirit of the Lord, fearlessly announcing God's punishment on Israel for her sins.

9 Listen to me, you leaders of Israel who hate justice and love unfairness,

10 And fill Jerusalem with murder and sin of every kind—

11 You leaders who take bribes; you priests and prophets who won't preach and prophesy until

you're paid: (And yet you fawn upon the Lord and say, "All is well—the Lord is here among us. No harm can come to us.")

12 It is because of you that Jerusalem will be plowed like a field, and become a heap of rubble; the mountaintop where the temple stands will be overgrown with brush.

CHAPTER 4

But in the last days Mount Zion will be the most renowned of all the mountains of the world, praised by all nations; people from all over the world will make pilgrimages there.

2 "Come," they will say to one another, "let us visit the mountain of the Lord, and see the temple of the God of Israel; He will tell us what to do, and we will do it." For in those days the whole world will be ruled by the Lord from Jerusalem! He will issue His laws and announce His decrees from there.

3 He will arbitrate among the nations, and dictate to strong nations far away. They will beat their swords into plowshares and their spears into pruning-hooks; nations shall no longer fight each other, for all war will end. There will be universal peace, and all the military academies and training camps will be closed down.

4 Everyone will live quietly in his own home in peace and prosperity, for there will be nothing to fear. The Lord Himself has promised this.

5 (Therefore we will follow the Lord our God

forever and ever, even though all the nations around
us worship idols!)

6 In that coming day, the Lord says that He will
bring back His punished people—sick and lame
and dispossessed—

7 And make them strong again in their own land,
a mighty nation; and the Lord Himself shall be
their King from Mount Zion for ever.

8 Oh Jerusalem—the Watchtower of God's
people—your royal might and power will come back
to you again, just as before.

9 But for now, now you scream in terror. Where
is your king to lead you? He is dead! Where are
your wise men? All are gone! Pain has gripped you
like a woman in travail.

10 Writhe and groan in your terrible pain, oh
people of Zion; for you must leave this city and live
in the fields; you will be sent far away into exile in
Babylon. But there I will rescue you and free you
from the grip of your enemies.

11 True, many nations have gathered together
against you, calling for your blood, eager to destroy
you.

12 But they do not know My thoughts nor understand My plan; for the time will come when the
Lord will gather together the enemies of His people
like sheaves upon the threshing floor,

13 Helpless before Israel. Rise, thresh, oh daughter of Zion; I will give you horns of iron and hoofs
of brass and you will trample to pieces many people;
and you will give their wealth as offerings to the
Lord, the Lord of all the earth.

CHAPTER 5

Mobilize! The enemy lays siege to Jerusalem!
With a rod they shall strike the Judge of Israel on
the face.

2 Oh Bethlehem Ephratah, you are but a small
Judean village, yet you will be the birthplace of My
King who is alive from everlasting ages past!

3 God will abandon His people to their enemies
until the time of Israel's spiritual rebirth;* then at
last the exile remnants of Israel will rejoin their
brethren in their own land.

4 And He shall stand and feed His flock in the
strength of the Lord, in the majesty of the Name of
the Lord His God; and His people shall remain
there undisturbed, for He will be greatly honored
all around the world.

5 He will be our Peace. And when the Assyrian
invades our land and marches across our hills, He
will appoint seven shepherds to watch over us, eight
princes to lead us.

6 They will rule Assyria with drawn swords and
enter the gates of the land of Nimrod. He will deliver us from the Assyrians when they invade our
land.

7 Then the nation of Israel will refresh the world
like a gentle dew or the welcome showers of rain,

8 And Israel will be as strong as a lion. The nations will be like helpless sheep before her!

9 She will stand up to her foes; all her enemies
will be wiped out.

*literally, "until she who is in travail has brought forth."

10 At that same time, says the Lord, I will destroy all the weapons you depend on,

11 And tear down your walls and demolish the defenses of your cities.

12 I will put an end to all witchcraft—there will be no more fortune-tellers to consult;

13 And destroy all your idols—never again will you worship what you have made;

14 And I will abolish the heathen shrines from among you, and destroy the cities where your idol temples stand.

* * * *

15 And I will pour out My vengeance upon the nations who refuse to obey Me.

CHAPTER 6

Listen to what the Lord is saying to His people: Stand up and state your case against Me. Let the mountains and hills be called to witness your complaint.

2 And now, oh mountains, listen to the Lord's complaint! For He has a case against His people Israel! He will prosecute them to the full.

3 Oh My people, what have I done that makes you turn away from Me? Tell Me why your patience is exhausted! Answer Me!

4 For I brought you out of Egypt, and cut your chains of slavery; and I gave you Moses, Aaron, and Miriam to help you.

5 Don't you remember, oh My people, how Balak,
king of Moab, tried to destroy you through the
curse of Balaam, son of Beor, but I made him bless
you instead? That is the kindness I showed you
again and again. Have you no memory at all of
what happened at Acacia and Gilgal, and how I
blessed you there?

6 "How can we make up to You for what we've
done?" you ask. "Shall we bow before the Lord
with offerings of yearling calves?" Oh, no!

7 For if you offered Him thousands of rams and
ten thousands of rivers of olive oil—would that
please Him? Would He be satisfied? If you sacrificed your oldest child, would that make Him glad?
Then would He forgive your sins? Of course not!

8 No, He has told you what He wants, and this
is all it is: to be fair and just and merciful, and to
walk humbly with your God.

9 The Lord's voice calls out to all Jerusalem—
listen to the Lord if you are wise! The armies of
destruction are coming; the Lord is sending them.

10 For your sins are very great—is there to be
no end of getting rich by cheating? The homes of
the wicked are full of ungodly treasures and lying
scales.

11 Shall I say "Good!" to all your merchants with
their bags of false, deceitful weights? How could
God be just while saying that?

12 Your rich men are wealthy through extortion
and violence; your citizens are so used to lying that
their tongues can't tell the truth!

13 Therefore I will wound you! I will make your
hearts miserable for all your sins.

14 You will eat but never have enough; hunger
pangs and emptiness will still remain. And though
you try and try to save your money, it will come
to nothing at the end; and what little you succeed
in storing up I'll give to those who conquer you!*

15 You will plant crops but not harvest them;
you will press out the oil from the olives, and not get
enough to anoint yourself! You will trample the
grapes, but get no juice to make your wine.

16 The only commands you keep are those of
Omri; the only example you follow is that of Ahab!
Therefore I will make an awesome example of you—
I will destroy you. I will make you the laughing-
stock of the world; all who see you will snicker and
sneer!

* * * *

CHAPTER 7

Woe is me! It is as hard to find an honest man
as grapes and figs when harvest days are over. Not
a cluster to eat, not a single early fig, however
much I long for it! The good men have disappeared
from the earth; not one fair-minded man is left.
They are all murderers, turning against even their
own brothers.

3 They go at their evil deeds with both hands;
and how skilled they are in using them! The governor and judge alike demand bribes. The rich
man pays them off and tells them whom to ruin.
Justice is twisted between them.

4 Even the best of them are prickly as briars; the

*See Haggai 1:6.

straightest is more crooked than a hedge of thorns.
But your judgment day is coming swiftly now; your
time of punishment is almost here; confusion, destruction, and terror will be yours.

5 Don't trust anyone, not your best friend—not
even your wife!

6 For the son despises his father; the daughter
defies her mother; the bride curses her mother-in-
law. Yes, a man's enemies will be found in his own
home.

7 As for me, I look to the Lord for His help; I
wait for God to save me; He will hear me.

8 Do not rejoice against me, oh my enemy; for
though I fall, I will rise again! When I sit in darkness, the Lord Himself will be my Light.

9 I will be patient while the Lord punishes me,
for I have sinned against Him; then He will defend
me from my enemies, and punish them for all the
evil they have done to me. God will bring me out
of my darkness into the light, and I will see His
goodness.

10 Then my enemy will see that God is for me,
and be ashamed for taunting me, "Where is that
God of yours?" Now with my own eyes I see them
trampled down like mud in the street.

* * * *

11 Your cities, people of God, will be rebuilt,
much larger and more prosperous than before.

12 Citizens of many lands will come and honor
you—from Assyria to Egypt, and from Egypt to
the Euphrates, from sea to sea and from distant
hills and mountains.

13 But first comes terrible destruction to Israel* for the great wickedness of her people.

14 Oh Lord, come and rule Your people; lead Your flock; make them live in peace and prosperity; let them enjoy the fertile pastures of Bashan and Gilead as they did long ago.

15 "Yes," replies the Lord, "I will do mighty miracles for you, like those when I brought you out of slavery in Egypt.

16 All the world will stand amazed at what I will do for you, and be embarrassed at their puny might. They will stand in silent awe, deaf to all around them."

17 They will see what snakes they are, lowly as worms crawling from their holes. They will come trembling out from their fortresses to meet the Lord our God. They will fear Him; they will stand in awe.

18 Where is another God like You, who pardons the sins of the survivors among His people? You cannot stay angry with Your people, for You love to be merciful.

19 Once again You will have compassion on us. You will tread our sins beneath Your feet; You will throw them into the depths of the ocean!

20 You will bless us as You promised Jacob long ago. You will set Your love upon us, as You promised our father Abraham!

*literally, "But the land will be desolate because of its inhabitants."

Nahum

CHAPTER 1

This is the vision God gave to Nahum, who lived
in Elkosh, concerning the impending doom of
Nineveh:*
2 God is jealous over those He loves; that is why
He takes vengeance on those who hurt them. He
furiously destroys their enemies.
3 He is slow in getting angry, but when aroused
His power is incredible, and He does not easily forgive. He shows His power in the terrors of the cy-
clone and the raging storms; clouds are billowing
dust beneath His feet!
4 At His command the oceans and rivers become
dry sand; the lush pastures of Bashan and Carmel
fade away; the green forests of Lebanon wilt.
5 In His presence mountains quake and hills
melt; the earth crumbles and its people are destroyed.
6 Who can stand before an angry God? His fury
is like fire; the mountains tumble down before His
anger.
7 The Lord is good. When trouble comes, He is
the place to go! And He knows everyone who trusts
in Him!
8 But He sweeps away His enemies with an over-
whelming flood; He pursues them all night long.
9 What are you thinking of, Nineveh, to defy the
Lord? He will stop you with one blow; He won't
need to strike again.

*Nineveh was the Assyrian capital.

10 He tosses His enemies into the fire like a
tangled mass of thorns. They burst into flames like
straw.
11 Who is this king* of yours who dares to plot
against the Lord?
12 But the Lord is not afraid of him! "Though
he build his army millions strong," the Lord declares, "it will vanish.
Oh My people, I have punished you enough!
13 Now I will break your chains and release you
from the yoke of slavery to this Assyrian king."*
14 And to the king He says, "I have ordered an
end to your dynasty; your sons will never sit upon
your throne. And I will destroy your gods and
temples, and I will bury you! For how you stink
with sin!"
15 See, the messengers come running down the
mountains with glad news: "The invaders have
been wiped out and we are safe!" Oh Judah, proclaim a day of thanksgiving, and worship only the
Lord, as you have vowed. For this enemy from
Nineveh will never come again. He is cut off forever; he will never be seen again.

CHAPTER 2

Nineveh, you are finished!† You are already surrounded by enemy armies! Sound the alarm! Man
the ramparts! Muster your defenses, full force,
and keep a sharp watch for the enemy attack to begin!
2 For the land of the people of God lies empty

*implied from verse 1 and 3:18.

†This chapter predicts the events of the year 612 B.C. when the combined armies of the Babylonians and Medes sacked impregnable Nineveh.

and broken after your attacks but the Lord will restore their honor and power again!

3 Shields flash red in the sunlight! The attack begins! See their scarlet uniforms! See their glittering chariots moving forward side by side, pulled by prancing steeds!

4 Your own chariots race recklessly along the streets and through the squares, darting like lightning, gleaming like torches.

5 The king shouts for his officers; they stumble in their haste, rushing to the walls to set up their defenses.

6 But too late! The river gates are open! The enemy has entered! The palace is in panic!

7 The queen of Nineveh is brought out naked to the streets, and led away, a slave, with all her maidens weeping after her; listen to them mourn like doves, and beat their breasts!

8 Nineveh is like a leaking water tank! Her soldiers slip away, deserting her; she cannot hold them back. "Stop, stop," she shouts, but they keep on running.

9 Loot the silver! Loot the gold! There seems to be no end of treasures. Her vast, uncounted wealth is stripped away.

10 Soon the city is an empty shambles; hearts melt in horror; knees quake; her people stand aghast, pale-faced and trembling.

11 Where now is that great Nineveh, lion of the nations, full of fight and boldness, where even the old and feeble, as well as the young and tender, lived unafraid?

12 Oh, Nineveh, once mighty lion! You crushed

your enemies to feed your children and your wives, and filled your city and your homes with captured goods and slaves.

13 But now the Lord of hosts has turned against you. He destroys your weapons. Your chariots stand there, silent and unused. Your finest youth lie dead. Never again will you bring back slaves from conquered nations; never again will you rule the earth.

CHAPTER 3

Woe to Nineveh, City of Blood, full of lies, crammed with plunder.

2 Listen! Hear the crack of the whips as the chariots rush forward against her; wheels rumbling, horses' hoofs pounding, and chariots clattering as they bump wildly through the streets!

3 See the flashing swords and glittering spears in the upraised arms of the cavalry! The dead are lying in the streets—bodies, heaps of bodies, everywhere. Men stumble over them, scramble to their feet, and fall again.

4 All this because Nineveh sold herself to the enemies of God. The beautiful and faithless city, mistress of deadly charms, enticed the nations with her beauty, then taught them all to worship her false gods,* bewitching people everywhere.

5 "No wonder I stand against you," says the Lord of hosts; "and now all the earth will see your nakedness and shame.

*literally, "who betrays nations with her harlotries."

6 I will cover you with filth and show the world
how really vile you are."

7 All who see you will shrink back in horror:
"Nineveh lies in utter ruin." Yet no one anywhere
regrets your fate!

8 Are you any better than Thebes,* straddling
the Nile, protected on all sides by the River?

9 Ethiopia and the whole land of Egypt were her
mighty allies; and she could call on them for infinite
assistance, as well as Put and Libya.

10 Yet Thebes fell and her people were led off as
slaves; her babies were dashed to death against the
stones of the streets. Soldiers drew straws to see
who would get her officers as servants. All her
leaders were bound in chains.

11 Nineveh, too, will stagger like a drunkard and
hide herself in fear.

12 All your forts will fall. They will be devoured
like first-ripe figs that fall into the mouths of those
who shake the trees.

13 Your troops will be weak and helpless as
women. The gates of your land will be opened
wide to the enemy and set on fire and burned.

14 Get ready for the siege! Store up water!
Strengthen the forts! Prepare many bricks for re-
pairing your walls! Go into the pits to trample the
clay, and pack it in the molds!

15 But in the middle of your preparations, the

*Thebes was conquered by the Assyrians 51 years before this prophecy.

fire will devour you; the sword will cut you down;
the enemy will consume you like young locusts that
eat up everything before them. There is no escape,
though you multiply like grasshoppers.

16 Merchants, numerous as stars, filled your city
with vast wealth, but your enemies swarm like
locusts and carry it away.

17 Your princes and officials crowd together like
grasshoppers in the hedges in the cold; but all of
them will flee away and disappear, like locusts
when the sun comes up and warms the earth.

18 Oh Assyrian king, your princes lie dead in the
dust; your people are scattered across the mountains; there is no shepherd now to gather them.

19 There is no healing for your wound—it is far
too deep to cure. All who hear your fate will clap
their hands for joy; for where can one be found
who has not suffered from your cruelty?

Habakkuk

CHAPTER 1

This is the message that came to the prophet Habakkuk in a vision from God:

2 Oh Lord, how long must I call for help before You will listen? I shout to You in vain; there is no answer. "Help! Murder!" I cry, but no one comes to save.

3 Must I forever see this sin and sadness all around me? Wherever I look there is oppression and bribery and men who love to argue and to fight.

4 The law is not enforced and there is no justice given in the courts; for the wicked far outnumber the righteous, and bribes and trickery prevail.

5 The Lord replied: "Look! and be amazed! You will be astounded at what I am about to do! For I am going to do something in your own lifetime that you will have to see to believe.

6 I am raising a new force on the world scene, the Chaldeans,* a cruel and violent nation who will march across the world and conquer it.

7 They are notorious for their cruelty. They do as they like, and no one can interfere.

8 Their horses are swifter than leopards. They are a fierce people, more fierce than wolves at dusk. Their cavalry move proudly forward from a distant

*Chaldeans: a tribe of Semites living between Babylon and the Persian Gulf, who began to assert themselves against the Assyrians around 630 B.C., and 25 years later had mastered most of the Near East.

land; like eagles they come swooping down to
pounce upon their prey.

9 All opposition melts away before the terror of
their presence. They collect captives like sand.

10 They scoff at kings and princes, and scorn
their forts. They simply heap up dirt against their
walls and capture them!

11* They sweep past like wind and are gone; but
their guilt is deep, for they claim their power is
from their gods."

12 Oh Lord my God, my Holy One, You who are
Eternal—is Your plan in all of this to wipe us out?
Surely not! oh God our Rock, You have decreed the
rise of these Chaldeans to chasten and correct us
for our awful sins.

13 We are wicked, but they far more! Will You,
who cannot allow sin in any form, stand idly by
while they swallow us up? Should You be silent
while the wicked destroy those who are better than
they?

14 Are we but fish, to be caught and killed? Are
we but creeping things that have no leader to defend them from their foes?

15 Must we be strung up on their hooks and
dragged out in their nets, while they rejoice?

16 Then they will worship their nets! and burn
incense before them! "These are the gods who
make us rich," they'll say.

17 Will You let them get away with this forever?
Will they succeed forever in their heartless wars?

*The Hebrew text of this verse is very uncertain.

CHAPTER 2

I will climb my watchtower now, and wait to see what answer God will give to my complaint.

* * * *

2 And the Lord said to me, "Write My answer on a billboard,* large and clear, so that anyone can read it at a glance and rush to tell the others.

3 But these things I plan won't happen right away. Slowly, steadily, surely, the time approaches when the vision will be fulfilled. If it seems slow, do not despair, for these things will surely come to pass. Just be patient! They will not be overdue a single day!

4 Note this: Wicked men trust themselves alone (as these Chaldeans do)†—and fail; but the righteous man trusts in Me—and lives!‡

5 What's more, these arrogant Chaldeans are betrayed by all their wine, for it is treacherous. In their greed they have collected many nations, but like death and hell, they are never satisfied.

6 The time is coming when all their captives will taunt them, saying: "You robbers! At last justice has caught up with you! Now you will get your just deserts for your oppression and extortion!"

7 Suddenly your debtors will rise up in anger and turn on you and take all you have, while you stand trembling and helpless.

8 You have ruined many nations; now they will

*literally, "on the tablets."
†implied.
‡or, "shall live by his faithfulness."

ruin you. You murderers! You have filled the countryside with lawlessness and all the cities too.

9 Woe to you for getting rich by evil means, attempting to live beyond the reach of danger.

10 By the murders you commit, you have shamed your name and forfeited your lives.

11 The very stones in the walls of your homes cry out against you, and the beams in the ceilings echo what they say.

12 Woe to you who build cities with money gained from murdering and robbery!

13 Has not the Lord decreed that godless nations' gains will turn to ashes in their hands? They work so hard, but all in vain!

14 (The time will come when all the earth is filled, as the waters fill the sea, with an awareness of the glory of the Lord.)

15 Woe to you for making your neighboring lands reel and stagger like drunkards beneath your blows, and then gloating over their nakedness and shame.

16 Soon your own glory will be replaced by shame. Drink down God's judgment on yourselves. Stagger and fall!

17 You cut down the forests of Lebanon—now you will be cut down! You terrified the wild animals you caught in your traps—now terror will strike you because of all your murdering and violence in cities everywhere.

18 What profit was there in worshiping all your man-made idols? What a foolish lie that they

could help! What fools you were to trust what you
yourselves had made.
19 Woe to those who command their lifeless
wooden idols to arise and save them, who call out to
the speechless stone to tell them what to do. Can
images speak for God? They are overlaid with gold
and silver, but there is no breath at all inside!
20 But the Lord is in His holy temple; let all the
earth be silent before Him.

CHAPTER 3

This is the prayer of triumph* that Habakkuk
sang before the Lord:
2 Oh Lord, now I have heard Your report, and I
worship You in awe for the fearful things You are
going to do. In this time of our deep need, begin
again to help us, as You did in years gone by. Show
us Your power to save us. In Your wrath, remember mercy.
3 I see God moving across the deserts from
Mount Sinai.† His brilliant splendor fills the earth
and sky; His glory fills the heavens, and the earth is
full of His praise! What a wonderful God He is!
4 From His hands flash rays of brilliant light. He
rejoices‡ in His awesome power.
5 Pestilence marches before Him; plague follows
close behind.
6 He stops; He stands still for a moment gazing
at the earth. Then He shakes the nations, scattering

*literally, "according to Shigionoth"—thought by some to mean a mournful dirge.
†literally, "from Teman . . . from Mount Paran."
‡or, "He veils His power."

the everlasting mountains and leveling the hills.
His power is just the same as always!

7 I see the people of Cushan and of Midian in
mortal fear.

8, 9 *Was it in anger, Lord, You smote the rivers
and parted the sea? Were You displeased with
them? No, You were sending Your chariots of salvation! All saw Your power! Then springs burst
forth upon the earth at Your command!

10 The mountains watched and trembled. Onward swept the raging water. The mighty deep
cried out, announcing its surrender to the Lord.†

11 The lofty sun and moon began to fade, obscured by brilliance from Your arrows and the
flashing of Your glittering spear.

12 You marched across the land in awesome
anger, and trampled down the nations in Your
wrath.

13 You went out to save Your chosen people.
You crushed the head of the wicked and laid bare
his bones from head to toe.

14 You destroyed with their own weapons those
who came out like a whirlwind, thinking Israel
would be an easy prey.

15 Your horsemen marched across the sea; the
mighty waters piled high.

16 I tremble when I hear all this; my lips quiver
with fear. My legs give way beneath me and I

*literally, "Was the Lord displeased against the rivers? Were you angry with them? Was your wrath against their sin that you rode upon your horses? Your chariots were salvation. Your bow was pulled from its sheath and you put arrows to the string. You ribboned the earth with rivers."

†literally, "and lifts high its hands."

shake in terror. I will quietly wait for the day of trouble to come upon the people who invade us.

* * * *

17 Even though the fig trees are all destroyed, and there is neither blossom left nor fruit; and though the olive crops all fail, and the fields lie barren; even if the flocks die in the fields and the cattle barns are empty,

18 Yet I will rejoice in the Lord; I will be happy in the God of my salvation.

19 The Lord God is my Strength, and He will give me the speed of a deer and bring me safely over the mountains.

(A note to the choir director: When singing this ode, the choir is to be accompanied by stringed instruments.)

Zephaniah

CHAPTER 1

Subject: A message from the Lord.

To: Zephaniah (son of Cushi, grandson of Gedaliah, great-grandson of Amariah, and great-great-grandson of Hezekiah).

When: During the reign of Josiah (son of Amon) king of Judah.*

2 "I will sweep away everything in all your land," says the Lord. "I will destroy it to the ground.

3 I will sweep away both men and animals alike. Mankind and all the idols that he worships—all will vanish. Even the birds of the air and the fish in the sea will perish.

4 I will crush Judah and Jerusalem with My fist, and destroy every remnant of those who worship Baal; I will put an end to their idolatrous priests, so that even the memory of them will disappear.

5 They go up on their roofs and bow to the sun, moon and stars. They 'follow the Lord,' but worship Molech, too! I will destroy them.

6 And I will destroy those who formerly worshiped the Lord, but now no longer do, and those who never loved Him and never wanted to."

*Note: The Great Revival under King Josiah followed about 10 years after this prophecy, and then, a dozen years later, the deportation and exile. The prophet Jeremiah was active during this same period.

7 Stand in silence in the presence of the Lord.
For the awesome day of His judgment has come;
He has prepared a great slaughter of His people
and has chosen their executioners.*

8 "On that day of judgment I will punish the
leaders and princes of Judah, and all others wearing heathen clothing.†

9 Yes, I will punish those who follow heathen
customs and who rob and kill to fill their masters'
homes with evil gain of violence and fraud.

10 A cry of alarm will begin at the farthest gate
of Jerusalem, coming closer and closer until the
noise of the advancing army reaches the very top
of the hill where the city is built.

11 Wail in sorrow, you people of Jerusalem. All
your greedy businessmen, all your loan sharks—all
will die.

12 I will search with lanterns in Jerusalem's
darkest corners to find and punish those who sit
contented in their sins, indifferent to God, thinking
He will let them alone.

13 They are the very ones whose property will be
plundered by the enemy, whose homes will be ran-
sacked; they will never have a chance to live in the
new homes they have built. They will never drink
wine from the vineyards they have planted."

14 That terrible day is near. Swiftly it comes—a
day when strong men will weep bitterly.

15 It is a day of the wrath of God poured out; it

*literally, "He has prepared a sacrifice and sanctified his guests."
†i.e., showing their desire for foreign gods and foreign ways, and their contempt for the Lord.

is a day of terrible distress and anguish; a day of ruin and desolation, of darkness, gloom, clouds, blackness,
16 Trumpet calls and battle cries; down go the walled cities and strongest battlements!
17 "I will make you as helpless as a blind man
searching for a path, because you have sinned against the Lord; therefore your blood will be poured out into the dust and your bodies will lie there rotting on the ground."
18 Your silver and gold will be of no use to you
in that day of the Lord's wrath. You cannot ransom yourselves with it.* For the whole land will be devoured by the fire of His jealousy. He will make a speedy riddance of all the people of Judah.

CHAPTER 2

Gather together and pray, you shameless nation,
2 While there still is time—before judgment be-
gins, and your opportunity is blown away like chaff; before the fierce anger of the Lord falls and the terrible day of His wrath begins.
3 Beg Him to save you, all who are humble—all
who have tried to obey. Walk humbly and do what is right; perhaps even yet the Lord will protect you from His wrath in that day of doom.
4 Gaza, Ashkelon, Ashdod, Ekron—these Philis-
tine cities, too, will be rooted out and left in desolation.
5 And woe to you Philistines† living on the coast

*implied.

†literally, "Cherethites (or Cretans)." With the Philistines, they were part of a great wave of immigrants to the southern coast of Palestine around 1200 B.C.

and in the land of Canaan; for the judgment is
against you, too. The Lord will destroy you until
not one of you is left.

6 The coastland will become a pasture, a place
of shepherd camps and folds for sheep.

7 There the little remnant of the tribe of Judah
will be pastured. They will lie down to rest in the
abandoned houses in Ashkelon. For the Lord God
will visit His people in kindness and restore their
prosperity again.

* * * *

8 "I have heard the taunts of the people of Moab
and Ammon, mocking My people and invading their
land.

9 Therefore as I live," says the Lord of Hosts,
God of Israel, "Moab and Ammon will be destroyed
like Sodom and Gomorrah, and become a place of
stinging nettles and salt pits and eternal desolation;
those of My people who are left will plunder and
possess them."

10 They will receive the wages of their pride, for
they have scoffed at the people of the Lord of Hosts.

11 The Lord will do terrible things to them. He
will starve out all these gods of foreign powers; and
everyone shall worship Him, each in his own land
throughout the world.

12 You Ethiopians, too, will be slain by His
sword,

13 And so will the lands of the north; He will
destroy Assyria and make its great capital Nineveh
a desolate wasteland like a wilderness.

14 That once proud city will become a pasture-
land for sheep. All sorts of wild animals will have
their homes in her. Hedgehogs will burrow there;

the vultures and the owls will live among the ruins of her palaces, hooting from the gaping windows; the ravens will croak from her doors. All her cedar paneling will lie open to the wind and weather.

15 This is the fate of that vast, prosperous city that lived in such security; that said to herself, "In all the world there is no city as great as I." But now—see how she has become a place of utter ruins, a place for animals to live! Everyone passing that way will mock, or shake his head in disbelief.*

CHAPTER 3

Woe to filthy, sinful Jerusalem, city of violence and crime.

2 In her pride she won't listen even to the voice of God. No one can tell her anything; she refuses all correction. She does not trust the Lord, nor seek for God.

3 Her leaders are like roaring lions hunting for their victims—out for everything that they can get. Her judges are like ravenous wolves at evening time, who by dawn have left no trace of their prey.

4 Her "prophets" are liars seeking their own gain; her priests defile the temple by their disobedience to God's laws.

5 But the Lord is there within the city, and He does no wrong. Day by day His justice is more evident, but no one heeds—the wicked know no shame.

*"Nothing then seemed more improbable than that the capital of so vast an empire, a city 60 miles around with walls 100 feet high and so thick that three chariots could go abreast on them, and with 1500 towers, should be so totally destroyed that its site is with difficulty discovered."
—Jamieson, Fausset and Brown Commentary

6 "I have cut off many nations, laying them waste to their farthest borders; I have left their streets in silent ruin and their cities deserted without a single survivor to remember what happened.

7 I thought, 'Surely they will listen to Me now—surely they will heed My warnings, so that I'll not need to strike again.' But no; however much I punish them, they continue all their evil ways from dawn to dusk and dusk to dawn."

8 But the Lord says, "Be patient; the time is coming soon when I will stand up and accuse these evil nations. For it is My decision to gather together the kingdoms of the earth, and pour out My fiercest anger and wrath upon them. All the earth shall be devoured with the fire of My jealousy.

9 At that time I will change the speech of My returning people to pure Hebrew* so that all can worship the Lord together.

10 Those who live far beyond the rivers of Ethiopia will come with their offerings, asking Me to be their God again.

11 And then you will no longer need to be ashamed of yourselves, for you will no longer be rebels against Me. I will remove all your proud and arrogant men from among you; there will be no pride or haughtiness on My holy mountain.

12 Those who are left will be the poor and the humble, and they will trust in the Name of the Lord.

13 They will not be sinners, full of lies and deceit.

*literally, ". . . I will change the speech of the peoples to a pure speech . . ." See Isaiah 19:18.

They will live quietly, in peace, and lie down in safety, and no one will make them afraid."

14 Sing, oh daughter of Zion; shout, oh Israel; be glad and rejoice with all your heart, oh daughter of Jerusalem.

15 For the Lord will remove His hand of judgment, and disperse the armies of your enemy. And the Lord Himself, the King of Israel, will live among you! At last your troubles will be over—you need fear no more.

16 On that day the announcement to Jerusalem will be, "Cheer up, don't be afraid.

17, 18 For the Lord your God has arrived to live among you. He is a mighty Savior. He will give you victory. He will rejoice over you in great gladness; He will love you and not accuse you." Is that a joyous choir I hear? No, it is the Lord Himself exulting over you in happy song:

"I have gathered your wounded and taken away your reproach.

19 And I will deal severely with all who have oppressed you. I will save the weak and helpless ones, and bring together those who were chased away. I will give glory to My former exiles, mocked and shamed.

20 At that time, I will gather you together and bring you home again, and give you a good name, a name of distinction among all the peoples of the earth; and they will praise you when I restore your fortunes before your very eyes," says the Lord.

Haggai

CHAPTER 1

Subject: A message from the Lord.

To: Haggai the prophet, who delivered it to Zerubbabel (son of Shealtiel), governor of Judah; and to Joshua (son of Josedech), the high priest—for it was addressed to them.*

When: In late August of the second year of the reign of King Darius I.

2 "Why is everyone saying it is not the right time for rebuilding My temple?" asks the Lord.

3, 4 His reply to them is this: "Is it then the right time for you to live in luxurious homes, when the temple lies in ruins?

5 Look at the result:

6 You plant much but harvest little. You have scarcely enough to eat or drink, and not enough clothes to keep you warm. Your income disappears, as though you were putting it into pockets filled with holes!"

7 "Think it over," says the Lord of Hosts. "Consider how you have acted, and what has happened as a result!

8 Then go up into the mountains and bring down timber, and rebuild My temple; and I will be pleased with it and appear there in My glory," says the Lord.

*Note: They were among the exiles who had returned from Babylon to rebuild Jerusalem.

9 "You hope for much but get so little. And when you bring it home, I blow it away—it doesn't last at all. Why? Because My temple lies in ruins and you don't care. Your only concern is your own fine homes.

10 That is why I am holding back the rains from heaven and giving you such scant crops.

11 In fact, I have called for a drought upon the land, yes, and in the highlands, too; a drought to wither the grain and grapes and olives and all your other crops; a drought to starve both you and all your cattle, and ruin everything you have worked so hard to get.

12 Then Zerubbabel (son of Shealtiel), the governor of Judah, and Joshua (son of Josedech), the high priest, and the few people remaining in the land obeyed Haggai's message from the Lord their God; they began to worship Him in earnest.

13 Then the Lord told them (again sending the message through Haggai, His messenger), "I am with you; I will bless you."

14, 15 And the Lord gave them a desire to rebuild His temple; so they all gathered in early September of the second year of King Darius' reign, and volunteered their help.

CHAPTER 2

In early October of the same year, the Lord sent them this message through Haggai:

2 Ask this question of the governor and high priest and everyone left in the land:

3 "Who among you can remember the temple as

it was before? How glorious it was? In comparison, it is nothing now, is it?

4 But take courage, oh Zerubbabel and Joshua and all the people; take courage and work, for 'I am with you,' says the Lord of Hosts.

5 'For I promised when you left Egypt that My Spirit would remain among you; so don't be afraid.'

6 For the Lord of Hosts says, 'In just a little while I will begin to shake the heavens and earth—and the oceans, too, and the dry land—

7 I will shake all nations; and the Desire of All Nations* shall come to this temple; and I will fill this place with My glory,' says the Lord of Hosts.

8, 9 'The future splendor of this temple will be greater than the splendor of the first one! For I have plenty of silver and gold to do it! And here I will give peace,'† says the Lord."

* * * *

10 In early December, in the second year of the reign of King Darius, this message came from the Lord through Haggai the prophet:

11 Ask the priests this question about the law:

12 "If one of you is carrying a holy sacrifice in his robes, and happens to brush against some bread or wine or meat, will it too become holy?"

"No," the priests replied. "Holiness does not pass to other things that way."

*i.e., Christ, the Messiah. Literally, "The Treasures" or "that which is choice." But many commentators prefer this rendering: "The treasures of the nations will pour into this temple, and I will fill it with splendor."

†Peace with God through Christ Who, 500 years later, came often to this temple.

13 Then Haggai asked, "But if someone touches a dead person, and so becomes ceremonially impure, and then brushes against something, does it become contaminated?" And the priests answered, "Yes."

14 Haggai then made his meaning clear. "You people," he said (speaking for the Lord), "were contaminating your sacrifices by living with selfish attitudes and evil hearts—and not only your sacrifices, but everything else that you did as a 'service' to me.

15 And so everything you did went wrong. But all is different now, because you have begun to build the temple.

16, 17 Before, when you expected a twenty bushel crop, there were only ten. When you came to draw fifty gallons from the olive press, there were only twenty. I rewarded all your labor with rust and mildew and hail. Yet, even so, you refused to return to Me," says the Lord.

18, 19 "But now note this: From today, this 24th day of the month,* as the foundation of the Lord's temple is finished, and from this day onward, I will bless you. Notice, I am giving you this promise now before you have even begun to rebuild the temple structure, and before you have harvested your grain, and before the grapes and figs and pomegranates and olives have produced their next crops: *from this day I will bless you.*"

* * * *

*"the 24th day of Kislev." This corresponds to early in our December.

20 Another message came to Haggai from the Lord that same day:

21 Tell Zerubbabel, the governor of Judah, "I am about to shake the heavens and the earth,

22 And to overthrow thrones and destroy the strength of the kingdoms of the nations. I will overthrow their armed might, and brothers and companions will kill each other.

23 But when that happens, I will take you, oh Zerubbabel My servant, and honor you like a signet ring upon My finger; for I have specially chosen you," says the Lord of Hosts.

Zechariah

CHAPTER 1

Subject: messages from the Lord.

These messages from the Lord were given to Zechariah (son of Berechiah, and grandson of Iddo the prophet) in early November of the second year of the reign of King Darius.

* * * *

2 The Lord of Hosts was very angry with your fathers.

3 But He will turn again and favor you if only you return to Him.

4 Don't be like your fathers were! The earlier prophets pled in vain with them to turn from all their evil ways. "Come, return to Me," the Lord God said, but no, they wouldn't listen; they paid no attention at all.

5, 6 Your fathers and their prophets are now long dead, but remember the lesson they learned, that *God's word endures!* It caught up with them and punished them. Then at last they repented. "We have gotten what we deserved from God," they said. "He has done just what He warned us He would."

* * * *

7 The following February, still in the second year of the reign of King Darius, another message from the Lord came to Zechariah (son of Berechiah and grandson of Iddo the prophet), in a vision in the night:

8 I saw a man sitting on a red horse that was standing among the myrtle trees beside a river. Behind him were other horses, red and bay and white, each with its rider.*

9 An angel stood beside me, and I asked him, "Sir, what are all those horses for?"

"I'll tell you," he replied.

10 Then the rider on the red horse—he was the Angel of the Lord—answered me, "The Lord has sent them to patrol the earth for Him."

11 Then the other riders reported to the Angel of the Lord, "We have patrolled the whole earth, and everywhere there is prosperity and peace."

12 Upon hearing this, the Angel of the Lord prayed this prayer: "Oh Lord of Hosts, for seventy years Your anger has raged against Jerusalem and the cities of Judah. How long will it be until You again show mercy to them?"

13 And the Lord answered the angel who stood beside me, speaking words of comfort and assurance.

14 Then the angel said, "Shout out this message from the Lord of Hosts: Don't you think I care about what has happened to Judah and Jerusalem? I am as jealous as a husband for his captive wife.

15 I am very angry with the heathen nations sitting around at ease; for I was only a little displeased with My people, but the nations afflicted them far beyond My intentions.

16 Therefore the Lord declares: I have returned

*implied.

to Jerusalem filled with mercy; My temple will be
rebuilt, says the Lord of Hosts and so will all
Jerusalem.
17 Say it again: the Lord of Hosts declares that
the cities of Israel will again overflow with prosperity, and the Lord will again comfort Jerusalem
and bless her and live in her."
18 Then I looked and saw four animal horns!
19 "What are these?" I asked the angel.
He replied, "They represent the four world
powers that have scattered Judah, Israel and Jerusalem."
20 Then the Lord showed me four blacksmiths.
21 "What have these men come to do?" I asked.
The angel replied, "They have come to take
hold of the four horns that scattered Judah so terribly, and to pound them on the anvil and throw
them away."

CHAPTER 2

When I looked around me again, I saw a man
carrying a yardstick in his hand.
2 "Where are you going?" I asked.
"To measure Jerusalem," he said; "I want to
see whether it is big enough for all the people!"
3 Then the angel who was talking to me went
over to meet another angel coming toward him.
4 "Go tell this young man," said the other angel,
"that Jerusalem will some day be so full of people
that she won't have room enough for all! Many
will live outside the city walls, with all their many
cattle—and yet they will be safe.
5 For the Lord Himself will be a wall of fire pro-

tecting them and all Jerusalem; He will be the glory
of the city.

6, 7 'Come, flee from the land of the north, from
Babylon,' says the Lord to all His exiles there; 'I
scattered you to the winds but I will bring you back
again. Escape, escape to Zion now!' says the Lord.

8 The Lord of Glory has sent Me* against the
nations that oppressed you, for he who harms you
sticks his finger in Jehovah's eye!

9 'I will smash them with My fist and their slaves
will be their rulers! *Then you will know it was the
Lord of Hosts who sent Me.*

10 Sing, Jerusalem, and rejoice! For I have come
to live among you,' says the Lord.

11, 12 'At that time many nations will be converted to the Lord, and they too shall be My
people; I will live among them all. *Then you will
know it was the Lord of Hosts who sent Me to you.*
And Judah shall be the Lord's inheritance in the
Holy Land, for God shall once more choose to bless
Jerusalem.'

13 Be silent, all mankind, before the Lord; for
He has come to earth from heaven, from His holy
home."

CHAPTER 3

Then the angel showed me (in my vision) Joshua
the high priest standing before the Angel of the
Lord; and Satan was there too, at the Angel's right
hand, accusing Joshua of many things.

*This passage evidently refers to the Messiah, here seen as one of the Godhead.

2 And the Lord said to Satan, "I reject your accusations,* Satan; yes, I, the Lord, for I have decided to be merciful to Jerusalem—I rebuke you. I have decreed mercy to Joshua and his nation; they are like a burning stick pulled out of the fire."

3 Joshua's clothing was filthy as he stood before the Angel of the Lord.

4 Then the Angel said to the others standing there, "Remove his filthy clothing." And turning to Joshua He said, "See, I have taken away your sins; and now I am giving you these fine new clothes."

5, 6 Then I said, "Please, could he also have a clean turban on his head?" So they gave him one. Then the Angel of the Lord spoke very solemnly to Joshua and said,

7 "The Lord of Hosts declares: 'If you will follow the paths I set for you and do all I tell you to, then I will put you in charge of My temple, to keep it holy; and I will let you walk in and out of My presence with these angels.

8 Listen to Me, oh Joshua the high priest, and all you other priests, you are illustrations of the good things to come. Don't you see?—Joshua represents My Servant The Branch† whom I will send.

9 He will be the Foundation Stone of the temple that Joshua is standing beside, and I will engrave this inscription on it seven times:‡ *I will remove the sins of this land in a single day.*

*literally, "The Lord rebuke you, oh Satan; even the Lord, who has chosen Jerusalem, rebuke you. Is not this a brand plucked out of the fire?"

†i.e., the Messiah, Christ.

‡literally, "See the stone with seven facets I have set before Joshua; and I will engrave its inscription."

10 And after that,' the Lord of Hosts declares, 'you will all live in peace and prosperity and each of you will own a home of your own where you can invite your neighbors.' "

CHAPTER 4

Then the angel who had been talking with me woke me, as though I had been asleep.

2 "What do you see now?" he asked.

I answered, "I see a golden lampstand holding seven lamps, and at the top there is a reservoir for the olive oil that feeds the lamps, flowing into them through seven tubes.

3 And I see two olive trees carved upon the lampstand, one on each side of the reservoir.

4 What is it, sir?" I asked. "What does this mean?"

5 "Don't you really know?" the angel asked.

"No, sir," I said, "I don't."

6 Then he said, "This is God's message to Zerubbabel:* 'Not by might, nor by power, but by My Spirit, says the Lord of Hosts—you will succeed because of My Spirit, though you are few and weak.'

7 Therefore no mountain, however high, can stand before Zerubbabel! For it will flatten out before him! And Zerubbabel will finish building this temple† with mighty shouts of thanksgiving for God's mercy, declaring that all was done by grace alone."‡

*Governor of Judah, who was given the responsibility for rebuilding the temple. See Haggai 1:1; 2:23, etc.

†literally, "He will bring forth the capstone."

‡or, "with mighty shouts, 'How beautiful it is;' " or, "the Lord bless it!"

* * * *

8 Another message that I received from the Lord said:

9 "Zerubbabel laid the foundation of this temple, and he will complete it. (Then you will know these messages are from God, the Lord of Hosts.)

10 Do not despise this small beginning, for the eyes of the Lord rejoice to see the work begin, to see the plumbline in the hand of Zerubbabel.

For these seven lamps represent the eyes of the Lord that see everywhere around the world."

11 Then I asked him about the two olive trees on each side of the lampstand,

12 And about the two olive branches that emptied oil into golden bowls through two golden tubes.

13 "Don't you know?" he asked.

"No, sir," I said.

14 Then he told me, "They represent the two anointed ones who assist the Lord of all the earth."

CHAPTER 5

I looked up again and saw a scroll flying through the air.

2 "What do you see?" he asked.

"A flying scroll!" I replied. "It appears to be about thirty feet long and fifteen feet wide!"

3 "This scroll," he told me, "represents the words of God's curse going out over the entire land. It says that all who steal and lie have been judged and sentenced to death."

4 "I am sending this curse into the home of every thief and everyone who swears falsely by My Name," says the Lord of Hosts. "And My curse shall remain upon his home and completely destroy it."

5 Then the angel left me for awhile, but he returned and said, "Look up! Something is traveling through the sky!"

6 "What is it?" I asked.

He replied, "It is a bushel basket filled with the sin prevailing everywhere throughout the land."

7 Suddenly the heavy lead cover on the basket was lifted off, and I could see a woman sitting inside the basket!

8 He said, "She represents wickedness," and he pushed her back into the basket and clamped down the heavy lid again.

9 Then I saw two women flying toward us, with wings like those of a stork. And they took the bushel basket and flew off with it, high in the sky.

10 "Where are they taking her?" I asked the angel.

11 He replied, "To Babylon* where she belongs and where she will stay!"

CHAPTER 6

Then I looked up again and saw four chariots coming from between what looked like two mountains made of brass.

*Babylon had, by the time of Zechariah, become a symbol, the center of world idolatry and wickedness.

2 The first chariot was pulled by red horses, the
second by black ones,

3 The third by white horses and the fourth by
dapple-greys.

4 "And what are these, sir?" I asked the angel.

5 He replied, "These are the four heavenly spirits
who stand before the Lord of all the earth; they
are going out to do His work.

6 The chariot pulled by the black horses will go
north, and the one pulled by white horses will follow it there,* while the dappled-greys will go
south."

7 The red† horses were impatient to be off, to
patrol back and forth across the earth, so the Lord
said, "Go. Begin your patrol." So they left at
once.

8 Then the Lord summoned me and said, "Those
who went north have executed My judgment and
quieted My anger there."

* * * *

9 In another message the Lord said:

10, 11 "Heldai, Tobijah and Jedaiah will bring
gifts of silver and gold from the Jews exiled in Babylon. The same day they arrive, meet them at the home of Josiah (son of Zephaniah), where they will stay. Accept their gifts and make from them a crown from the silver and gold. Then put the crown on the head of Joshua (son of Josedech) the high priest.

12 Tell him that the Lord of Hosts says, 'You
represent the Man who will come, whose name is

*or, "will go west."
†"red" implied.

The Branch—He will grow up from Himself*—and will build the temple of the Lord.

13 To Him belongs the royal title. He will rule both as King and as Priest, with perfect harmony between the two!'

14 Then put the crown in the temple of the Lord, to honor those who gave it—Heldai, Tobijah, Jedaiah, and also Josiah.

15 These three who have come from so far away represent many others who will some day come from distant lands to rebuild the temple of the Lord. And when this happens you will know my messages have been from God, the Lord of Hosts. But none of this will happen unless you carefully obey the commandments of the Lord your God."

CHAPTER 7

Another message came to me from the Lord in late November of the fourth year of the reign of King Darius.

2 The Jews of the city of Bethel had sent a group of men headed by Sharezer, the chief administrative officer of the king, and Regemmelech, to the Lord's temple at Jerusalem, to seek His blessing,

3 And to speak with the priests and prophets about whether they must continue their traditional custom of fasting and mourning during the month of August each year, as they had been doing so long.

4 This was the Lord's reply:

*literally, "He will grow up in His place."

5 "When you return to Bethel, say to all your
people and your priests, 'During those seventy years
of exile when you fasted and mourned in August
and October, were you really in earnest about
leaving your sins behind, and coming back to Me?
No, not at all!

6 And even now in your holy feasts to God, you
don't think of Me, but only of the food and fellowship and fun.

7 Long years ago, when Jerusalem was prosperous and her southern suburbs out along the plain
were filled with people, the prophets warned them
that this attitude would surely lead to ruin, as it
has.' "

* * * *

8, 9 Then this message from the Lord came to
Zechariah. "Tell them to be honest and fair—and
not to take bribes—and to be merciful and kind to
everyone.

10 Tell them to stop oppressing widows and orphans, foreigners and poor people; and to stop plotting evil against each other.

11 Your fathers would not listen to this message.
They turned stubbornly away and put their fingers
in their ears to keep from hearing Me.

12 They hardened their hearts like flint, afraid to
hear the words that God, the Lord of Hosts, commanded them—the laws He had revealed to them
by His Spirit through the early prophets. That is
why such great wrath came down on them from
God.

13 I called but they refused to listen; so when
they cried to Me, I turned away.

14 I scattered them as with a whirlwind among

the far-off nations. Their land became desolate; no one even traveled through it; the Pleasant Land lay bare and blighted."

CHAPTER 8

1 Again the Lord's message came to me:

2 "The Lord of Hosts says, I am greatly concerned—yes, furiously angry—because of all that Jerusalem's enemies have done to her.

3 Now I am going to return to My land and I, Myself, will live within Jerusalem; and Jerusalem shall be called 'The Faithful City,' and 'The Holy Mountain,' and 'The Mountain of the Lord of Hosts.' "

4 The Lord of Hosts declares that Jerusalem will have peace and prosperity so long that there will once again be aged men and women hobbling through her streets on canes;

5 And the streets will be filled with boys and girls at play.

6 The Lord says, "This seems unbelievable to you—a remnant, small, discouraged as you are—but it is no great thing for Me.

7 You can be sure that I will rescue My people from east and west, wherever they are scattered.

8 I will bring them home again to live safely in Jerusalem; and they will be My people, and I will be their God, just and true and yet forgiving them their sins*!"

9 The Lord of Hosts says, "Get on with the job

*literally, "I will be their God in truth and in righteousness."

and finish it! You have been listening long enough! For since you began laying the foundation of the temple, the prophets have been telling you about the blessings that await you when it's finished.

10 Before the work began there were no jobs, no wages, no security; if you left the city, there was no assurance you would ever return, for crime was rampant.

11 But it is all so different now!" says the Lord of Hosts.

12 "For I am sowing peace and prosperity among you. Your crops will prosper; the grapevines will be weighted down with fruit; the ground will be fertile, with plenty of rain; all these blessings will be given to the people left in the land.

13 'May you be as poor as Judah,' the heathen used to say to those they cursed! But no longer! For now 'Judah' is a word of blessing, not a curse. 'May you be as prosperous and happy as Judah is,' they'll say. So don't be afraid or discouraged! Get on with rebuilding the temple!

14, 15 If you do, I will certainly bless you. And don't think that I might change My mind. I did what I said I would when your fathers angered Me and I promised to punish them; and I won't change this decision of Mine to bless you.

16 Here is your part: Tell the truth. Be fair. Live at peace with everyone.

17 Don't plot harm to others; don't swear that something is true when it isn't! How I hate all that sort of thing!" says the Lord.

* * * *

18 Here is another message that came to me from the Lord of Hosts:

19 "The traditional fasts and times of mourning you have kept in July, August, October, and January* are ended. They will be changed to joyous festivals if you love truth and peace!

20, 21 People from around the world will come on pilgrimages and pour into Jerusalem from many foreign cities to attend these celebrations. People will write their friends in other cities and say, 'Let's go to Jerusalem to ask the Lord to bless us, and be merciful to us. I'm going! Please come with me. Let's go *now!*'

22 Yes, many people, even strong nations, will come to the Lord of Hosts in Jerusalem to ask for His blessing and help.

23 In those days ten men from ten different nations will clutch at the coat sleeves of one Jew and say, 'Please be my friend, for I know that God is with you.' "

CHAPTER 9

This is the message concerning God's curse on the lands of Hadrach and Damascus; for the Lord is closely watching all mankind,† as well as Israel.

2 "Doomed is Hamath, near Damascus, and Tyre, and Zidon, too, shrewd though they be.

*literally, "fourth, fifth, seventh, and tenth months."

†or, "for the cities of Syria belong to the Lord, as much as to the tribes of Israel."

3 Though Tyre has armed herself to the hilt, and become so rich that silver is like dirt to her, and fine gold like dust in the streets,

4 Yet the Lord will dispossess her, and hurl her fortifications into the sea; and she shall be set on fire and burned to the ground.

5 Ashkelon will see it happen and be filled with fear; Gaza will huddle in desperation and Ekron will shake with terror, for their hopes that Tyre would stop the enemies' advance will all be dashed. Gaza will be conquered, her king killed; and Ashkelon will be completely destroyed.

6 Foreigners will take over the city of Ashdod, the rich city of the Philistines.

7 I will yank her idolatry out of her mouth, and pull from her teeth her sacrifices that she eats with blood. Everyone left will worship God and be adopted into Israel as a new clan: the Philistines of Ekron will intermarry with the Jews, just as the Jebusites did so long ago.

8 And I will surround My temple like a guard to keep invading armies from entering Israel. I am closely watching their movements and I will keep them away; no foreign oppressors will again overrun My people's land.

9 Rejoice greatly, oh My people! Shout with joy! For look—your King is coming! He is the Righteous One, the Victor! yet He is lowly, riding on a donkey's colt!

10 I will disarm all peoples of the earth, including
My people in Israel, and He shall bring peace
among the nations. His realm shall stretch from
sea to sea, from the river to the ends of the earth.*

11 I have delivered you from death in a waterless
pit, because of the covenant I made with you, sealed
with blood.

12 Come to the place of safety, all you prisoners;
for there is yet hope! I promise right now, I will
repay you two mercies for each of your woes!

13 Judah, you are My bow! Ephraim, you are
My arrow! Both of you will be My sword, like the
sword of a mighty soldier brandished against the
sons of Greece."

14 The Lord shall lead His people as they fight!
His arrows shall fly like lightning; the Lord God
shall sound the trumpet call and go out against His
enemies like a whirlwind off the desert from the
south.

15 He will defend His people and they will subdue
their enemies, treading them beneath their feet.
They will taste victory and shout with triumph.
They will slaughter their foes, leaving horrible car-
nage everywhere.

16, 17 The Lord their God will save His people
in that day, as a Shepherd caring for His sheep.
They shall shine in His land as glittering jewels in
a crown. How wonderful and beautiful all shall be!
The abundance of grain and wine will make the
young men and girls flourish; they will be radiant
with health and happiness.

*or, "to the ends of the land" of Palestine. Either interpretation is possible from the Hebrew text, but many other passages indicate Christ's universal rule.

CHAPTER 10

Ask the Lord for rain in the springtime, and He will answer with lightning and showers. Every field will become a lush pasture.

2 How foolish to ask the idols for anything like that! Fortune-tellers' predictions are all a bunch of silly lies; what comfort is there in promises that don't come true? Judah and Israel have been led astray and wander like lost sheep; everyone attacks them, for they have no shepherd to protect them.

3 "My anger burns against your 'shepherds'—your leaders—and I will punish them—these goats. For the Lord of Hosts has arrived to help His flock of Judah. I will make them strong and glorious like a proud steed in battle.

4 From them will come the Cornerstone, the Peg on which all hope hangs, the Bow that wins the battle, the Ruler over all the earth.*

5 They will be mighty warriors for God, grinding their enemies' faces into the dust beneath their feet. The Lord is with them as they fight; their enemy is doomed.

6 I will strengthen Judah, yes, and Israel too; I will re-establish them because I love them. It will be as though I had never cast them all away, for I, the Lord their God, will hear their cries.

7 They shall be like mighty warriors. They shall be happy as with wine. Their children, too, shall see the mercies of the Lord and be glad. Their hearts shall rejoice in the Lord.

*i.e., the Messiah.

8 When I whistle to them, they'll come running, for I have bought them back again. From the few that are left, their population will grow again to former size.

9 Though I have scattered them like seeds among the nations, still they will remember Me and return again to God; with all their children, they will come home again to Israel.

10 I will bring them back from Egypt and Assyria, and resettle them in Israel—in Gilead and Lebanon; there will scarcely be room for all of them!

11 They shall pass safely through the sea of distress,* for the waves will be held back. The Nile will become dry—the rule of Assyria and Egypt over My people will end."

12 The Lord says, "I will make My people strong with power from Me! They will go wherever they wish; and wherever they go, they will be under My personal care."

CHAPTER 11

Open your doors, oh Lebanon, to judgment.† You will be destroyed as though by fire raging through your forests.

2 Weep, oh cypress trees, for all the ruined cedars; the tallest and most beautiful of them are fallen. Cry in fear, you oaks of Bashan, as you watch the thickest forests felled.

*or, "the Sea of Egypt," referring to the Red Sea which the people of Israel were miraculously brought through when God brought them out of slavery the first time.

†implied.

3 Listen to the wailing of Israel's leaders—all these evil shepherds—for their wealth is gone. Hear the young lions roaring—the princes are weeping, for their glorious Jordan valley lies in ruins.

* * * *

4 Then said the Lord my God to me, "Go and take a job as shepherd of a flock being fattened for the butcher.

5 This will illustrate the way My people have been bought and slain by wicked leaders, who go unpunished. 'Thank God, now I am rich!' say those who have betrayed them—their own shepherds have sold them without mercy.

6 And I won't spare them either," says the Lord, "for I will let them fall into the clutches of their own wicked leaders, and they will slay them. They shall turn the land into a wilderness and I will not protect it from them."

7 So I took two shepherd's staffs, naming one "Grace" and the other "Union," and I fed the flock as I had been told to do.

8 And I got rid of their three evil shepherds in a single month. But I became impatient with these sheep—this nation—and they hated me too.

9 So I told them, "I won't be your shepherd any longer. If you die, you die; if you are killed, I don't care. Go ahead and destroy yourselves!"

10 And I took my staff called "Grace" and snap-

ped it in two, showing that I had broken my contract to lead and protect them.

11 That was the end of the agreement. Then those who bought and sold sheep, who were watching, realized that God was telling them something through what I did.

12 And I said to their leaders, "If you like, give me my pay, whatever I am worth; but only if you want to." So they counted out thirty little silver coins* as my wages.

13 And the Lord told me, "Toss it into the temple treasury†—this magnificent sum they value you at!" So I took the thirty coins and threw them in.

14 Then I broke my other staff, "Union," to show that the bond of unity between Judah and Israel was broken.

15 Then the Lord told me to go again and get a job as a shepherd: this time I was to act the part of a worthless, wicked shepherd.

16 And He said to me, "This illustrates how I will give this nation a shepherd who will not care for the dying ones, nor look after the young, nor heal the broken bones, nor feed the healthy ones, nor carry the lame that cannot walk; instead, he will eat the fat ones, even tearing off their feet.

17 Woe to this worthless shepherd who doesn't care for the flock. God's sword will cut his arm and pierce through his right eye; his arm will become useless and his right eye blinded."

*The price of a slave. See Exodus 21:32; and Matthew 27:3-9.

†The translation here follows the Syriac version. "Cast it to the potter" is the Hebrew.

CHAPTER 12

This is the fate of Israel, as pronounced by the Lord, who stretched out the heavens and laid the foundation of the earth, and formed the spirit of man within him:

2 "I will make Jerusalem and Judah like a cup of poison to all the nearby nations that send their armies to surround Jerusalem.

3 Jerusalem will be a heavy stone burdening the world. And though all the nations of the earth unite in an attempt to move her, they will all be crushed.

4 In that day," says the Lord, "I will bewilder the armies drawn up against her, and make fools of them; for I will watch over the people of Judah, but blind all her enemies.

5 And the clans of Judah shall say to themselves, 'The people of Jerusalem have found strength in the Lord of Hosts, their God.'

6 In that day I will make the clans of Judah like a little fire that sets the forest aflame—like a burning match among the sheaves; they will burn up all the neighboring nations right and left, while Jerusalem stands unmoved.

7 The Lord will give victory to the rest of Judah first, before Jerusalem; so that the people of Jerusalem and the royal line of David won't be filled with pride at their success.

8 The Lord will defend the people of Jerusalem; the weakest among them will be as mighty as King

David! And the royal line will be as God, like the
Angel of the Lord who goes before them!

9 For My plan is to destroy all the nations that
come against Jerusalem.

10 Then I will pour out the spirit of grace and
prayer on all the people of Jerusalem; and they will
look on Him they pierced, and mourn for Him as for
an only son, and grieve bitterly for Him as for an
oldest child who died.

11 The sorrow and mourning in Jerusalem at
that time will be even greater than the grievous
mourning for the godly king Josiah,* who was killed
in the valley of Megiddo.

12, 13, 14 All of Israel will weep in profound sorrow. The whole nation will be bowed down with
universal grief—king, prophet, priest, and people.
Each family will go into private mourning, husband
and wife apart, to face their sorrow alone."

CHAPTER 13

At that time a Fountain will be opened to the
people of Israel and Jerusalem, a Fountain to
cleanse them from all their sins and uncleanness."

2 And the Lord of Hosts declares, "In that day I
will get rid of every vestige of idol worship throughout the land, so that even the names of the idols
will be forgotten. All false prophets and fortune-
tellers will be wiped out,

*Implied from II Chronicles 35:24, 25. Literally, "Like the mourning of Hadad-rimmon in the valley of Megiddo."

3 And if anyone begins false prophecy again, his own father and mother will slay him! 'You must die,' they will tell him, 'for you are prophesying lies in the name of the Lord.'

4 No one will be boasting then of his prophetic gift! No one will wear prophet's clothes to try to fool the people then.

5 'No,' he will say. 'I am not a prophet; I am a farmer. The soil has been my livelihood from my earliest youth.'

6 And if someone asks, 'Then what are these scars on your chest and your back?'* he will say, 'I got into a brawl at the home of a friend!'†

7 Awake, oh sword, against My Shepherd, the man who is my associate and equal," says the Lord of Hosts. "Strike down the Shepherd and the sheep will scatter; but I will come back and comfort and care for the lambs.

8 Two-thirds of all the nation of Israel will be cut off and die,‡ but a third will be left in the land.

9 I will bring the third that remain through the fire and make them pure, as gold and silver are refined and purified by fire. They will call upon My Name and I will hear them; I will say, 'These are My people,' and they will say, 'The Lord is our God.' "

*Evidently self-inflicted cuts, as practiced by false prophets. See I Kings 18:28.

†literally, "(These are) wounds I received in the house of my friends." That this is not a passage referring to Christ, is clear from the context. This is a false prophet who is lying about the reason for his scars.

‡This has already happened twice: two million Jews perished in the Roman wars, six million under Hitler. Is a yet future disaster foretold here?

CHAPTER 14

Watch, for the day of the Lord is coming soon!
On that day the Lord will gather together the nations to fight Jerusalem; and the city will be taken,
the houses rifled, the loot divided, the women raped;
half the population will be taken away as slaves,
and half will be left in what remains of the city.

3 Then the Lord will go out fully armed for war,
to fight against those nations.

4 That day His feet will stand upon the Mount
of Olives, to the east of Jerusalem; and the Mount
of Olives will split apart, making a very wide valley
running from east to west; for half the mountain
will move toward the north and half toward the
south.

5 You will escape through that valley, for it will
reach across to the city gate.* Yes, you will escape
as your people did long centuries ago from the
earthquake in the days of Uzziah, king of Judah;
and the Lord my God shall come, and all His saints
and angels† with Him.

6 The sun and moon and stars will no longer
shine,‡

7 Yet there will be continuous day! Only the
Lord knows how! There will be no normal day and
night—at evening time it will still be light.

8 Life-giving waters will flow out from Jerusalem,
half towards the Dead Sea and half towards the

*literally, "for the valley of My mountain shall touch Azel"—apparently a hamlet on the eastern outskirts of Jerusalem.
†literally, "His holy ones."
‡The Hebrew is uncertain.

Mediterranean, flowing continuously both in winter and in summer.

9 And the Lord shall be King over all the earth. In that day there shall be one Lord—His name alone will be worshiped.

10 All the land from Geba (the northern border of Judah) to Rimmon (the southern border) will become one vast plain, but Jerusalem will be on an elevated site, covering the area all the way from the Gate of Benjamin over to the site of the old gate, then to the Corner Gate, and from the Tower of Hananeel to the king's wine presses.

11 And Jerusalem shall be inhabited, safe at last, never again to be cursed and destroyed.

12 And the Lord will send a plague on all the people who fought Jerusalem. They will become like walking corpses, their flesh rotting away; their eyes will shrivel in their sockets, and the tongues will decay in their mouths.

13 They will be seized with terror, panic-stricken from the Lord, and will fight against each other in hand-to-hand combat.

14 All Judah will be fighting at* Jerusalem. The wealth of all the neighboring nations will be confiscated—great quantities of gold and silver and fine clothing.

15 (This same plague will strike the horses, mules, camels, donkeys, and all the other animals in the enemy camp.)

*or, "against Jerusalem."

16 In the end, those who survive the plague will go up to Jerusalem each year to worship the King, the Lord of Hosts; to celebrate a time* of thanksgiving.

17 And any nation anywhere in all the world that refuses to come to Jerusalem to worship the King, the Lord of Hosts, will have no rain.

18 But if Egypt refuses to come, God will punish her with some other plague.

19 And so Egypt and the other nations will all be punished if they refuse to come.

20 In that day the bells on the horses will have written on them, "These are Holy Property";† and the trash cans in the temple of the Lord will be as sacred as the bowls beside the altar.

21 In fact, every container in Jerusalem and Judah shall be sacred to the Lord of Hosts; all who come to worship may use any of them free of charge to boil their sacrifices in; there will be no more grasping traders in the temple of the Lord of Hosts!

*literally, "the Feast of Tabernacles" or "Booths."
†literally, "Holy to the Lord."

Malachi

CHAPTER 1

Here is the Lord's message to Israel, given
through the prophet Malachi:

2, 3 "I have loved you very deeply," says the
Lord. But you retort, "Really? When was this?"

And the Lord replies, "I showed My love for
you by loving your father, Jacob. I didn't need to.
I even rejected his very own brother, Esau, and destroyed Esau's mountains and inheritance, to give
it to the jackals of the desert.

4 And if his descendants should say, 'We will
rebuild the ruins,' then the Lord of Hosts will say,
'Try to if you like, but I will destroy it again,' for
their country is named The Land of Wickedness
and their people are called Those Whom God Does
Not Forgive."

5 Oh Israel, lift your eyes to see what God is doing
all around the world; then you will say, "Truly, the
Lord's great power goes far beyond our borders!"

6 "A son honors his father, a servant honors his
master. I am your Father and Master, yet you
don't honor Me, oh priests, but you despise My
Name."

"Who? Us?" you say. "When did we ever
despise Your Name?"

7 "When you offer polluted sacrifices on My
altar."

"Polluted sacrifices? When have we ever done
a thing like that?"

"Every time you say, 'Don't bother bringing anything very valuable to offer to God!'

8 You tell the people, 'Lame animals are all right to offer on the altar of the Lord—yes, even the sick and the blind ones.' And you claim this isn't evil? Try it on your governor sometime—give him gifts like that—and see how pleased he is!

9 'God have mercy on us,' you recite; 'God be gracious to us!' But when you bring that kind of gift, why should He show you any favor at all?

10 Oh, to find one priest among you who would shut the doors and refuse this kind of sacrifice. I have no pleasure in you," says the Lord of Hosts, "and I will not accept your offerings.

11 But My Name will be honored by the Gentiles from morning till night. All around the world they will offer sweet incense and pure offerings in honor of My Name. For My Name shall be great among the nations," says the Lord of Hosts.

12 "But you dishonor it, saying that My altar is not important, and encouraging people to bring cheap, sick animals to offer to Me on it.

13 You say, 'Oh, it's too difficult to serve the Lord and do what He asks.' And you turn up your noses at the rules He has given you to obey. Think of it! Stolen animals, lame and sick—as offerings to God! Should I accept such offerings as these?" asks the Lord.

14 "Cursed is that man who promises a fine ram from his flock, and substitutes a sick one to sacrifice to God. For I am a Great King," says the Lord of

Hosts, "and My Name is to be mightily revered among the Gentiles."

CHAPTER 2

Listen, you priests, to this warning from the Lord of Hosts:

2 "If you don't change your ways and give glory to My Name, then I will send terrible punishment upon you, and instead of giving you blessings as I would like to, I will turn on you with curses. Indeed, I have cursed you already because you haven't taken seriously the things that are most important to Me.

3 Take note that I will rebuke your children and I will spread on your faces the manure of these animals you offer Me, and throw you out like dung.

4 Then at last you will know it was I who sent you this warning to return to the laws I gave your father Levi," says the Lord of Hosts.

5 "The purpose of these laws was to give him life and peace, to be a means of showing his respect and awe for Me, by keeping them.

6 He passed on to the people all the truth he got from Me. He did not lie or cheat; he walked with Me, living a good and righteous life, and turned many from their lives of sin.

7 Priests' lips should flow with the knowledge of God so the people will learn God's laws. The priests are the messengers of the Lord of Hosts, and men should come to them for guidance.

8 But not to you! For you have left God's paths.

Your 'guidance' has caused many to stumble in sin. You have distorted the covenant of Levi, and made it into a grotesque parody," says the Lord of Hosts.

9 "Therefore I have made you contemptible in the eyes of all the people: for you have not obeyed Me, but you let your favorites break the law without rebuke."

* * * *

10 We are children of the same father, Abraham, all created by the same God. And yet we are faithless to each other, violating the covenant of our fathers!

11 In Judah, in Israel and in Jerusalem, there is treachery; for the men of Judah have defiled God's holy and beloved temple by marrying heathen women who worship idols.

12 May the Lord cut off from His covenant every last man, whether priest or layman, who has done this thing!

13 Yet you cover the altar with your tears because the Lord doesn't pay attention to your offerings anymore, and you receive no blessing from Him.

14 "Why has God abandoned us?" you cry. I'll tell you why: it is because the Lord has seen your treachery in divorcing your wives who have been faithful to you through the years, the companions you promised to care for and keep.

15 You were united to your wife by the Lord. In God's wise plan, when you married, the two of you became one person in His sight. And what does He want? Godly children from your union. Therefore guard your passions! Keep faith with the wife of your youth.

16 For the Lord, the God of Israel, says He hates divorce and cruel men. Therefore control your passions—let there be no divorcing of your wives.

17 You have wearied the Lord with your words.

"Wearied Him?" you ask in fake surprise. "How have we wearied Him?"

"By saying that evil is good, that it pleases the Lord! or by saying that God won't punish us—He doesn't care."

CHAPTER 3

Listen: I will send My messenger before Me to prepare the way. And then the One* you are looking for will come suddenly to His temple—the Messenger of God's promises, to bring you great joy. Yes, He is surely coming," says the Lord of Hosts.

2 "But who can live when He appears? Who can endure His coming? For He is like a blazing fire refining precious metal and He can bleach the dirtiest garments!

3 Like a refiner of silver He will sit and closely watch as the dross is burned away. He will purify the Levites, the ministers of God, refining them like gold or silver, so that they will do their work for God with pure hearts.

4 Then once more the Lord will enjoy the offerings brought to Him by the people of Judah and Jerusalem, as He did before.

5 At that time My punishments will be quick and certain; I will move swiftly against wicked men who trick the innocent, against adulterers, and

*literally, "the Lord."

liars, against all those who cheat their hired hands, or oppress widows and orphans, or defraud strangers, and do not fear Me," says the Lord of Hosts.

6 "For I am the Lord—I do not change. That is why you are not already utterly destroyed (for My mercy endures forever).*

7 Though you have scorned My laws from earliest time, yet you may still return to Me," says the Lord of Hosts. "Come and I will forgive you. But you say, 'We have never even gone away!'

8 Will a man rob God? Surely not! And yet you have robbed Me.

'What do you mean? When did we ever rob You?'

You have robbed Me of the tithes and offerings due to Me.

9 And so the awesome curse of God is cursing you, for your whole nation has been robbing Me.

10 Bring all the tithes into the storehouse so that there will be food enough in My temple; if you do, I will open up the windows of heaven for you and pour out a blessing so great you won't have room enough to take it in! Try it! Let Me prove it to you!

11 Your crops will be large, for I will guard them from insects and plagues. Your grapes won't shrivel away before they ripen," says the Lord of Hosts.

12 "And all nations will call you blessed, for you will be a land sparkling with happiness. These are the promises of the Lord of Hosts.

13 Your attitude toward Me has been proud and

*implied.

arrogant," says the Lord. "But you say, 'What do You mean? What have we said that we shouldn't?'

14, 15 Listen, you have said, 'It is foolish to worship God and obey Him. What good does it do to obey His laws, and to sorrow and mourn for our sins? From now on, as far as we're concerned, Blessed are the arrogant. For those who do evil shall prosper, and those who dare God to punish them shall get off scot-free.' "

* * * *

16 Then those who feared and loved the Lord spoke often of Him to each other. And He had a Book of Remembrance drawn up in which He recorded the names of those who feared Him and loved to think about Him.

17 "They shall be Mine," says the Lord of Hosts, "in that day when I make up My jewels. And I will spare them as a man spares an obedient and dutiful son.

18 Then you will see the difference between God's treatment of good men and bad, between those who serve Him and those who don't."

CHAPTER 4

Watch now," the Lord of Hosts declares, "the day of judgment is coming, burning like a furnace.

The proud and wicked will be burned up like straw; like a tree, they will be consumed—roots and all.

2 But for you who fear My Name, the Sun of Righteousness will rise with healing in His wings. And you will go free, leaping with joy like calves let out to pasture.

3 Then you will tread upon the wicked as ashes underfoot," says the Lord of Hosts.

4 "Remember to obey the laws I gave all Israel through Moses My servant on Mount Horeb.

5 See, I will send you another prophet like* Elijah before the coming of the great and dreadful judgment day of God.

6 His preaching will bring fathers and children together again, to be of one mind and heart, for they will know that if they do not repent, I will come and utterly destroy their land."

*literally, "the prophet Elijah." Compare Matthew 17:10-12 and Luke 1:17.

The Revelation

CHAPTER 1

This book unveils some of the future activities soon to occur in the life of Jesus Christ.* God permitted Him to reveal these things to His servant John in a vision; and then an angel was sent from heaven to explain the vision's meaning.

2 John wrote it all down—the words of God and Jesus Christ and everything he heard and saw.

3 If you read this prophecy aloud to the church, you will receive a special blessing from the Lord. Those who listen to it being read and do what it says will also be blessed. For the time is near when these things will all come true.

* * * *

4 *From:* John

To: The seven churches in Turkey.†

Dear Friends:

May you have grace and peace from God who is, and was, and is to come! and from the seven-fold Spirit‡ before His throne;

5 And from Jesus Christ who faithfully reveals all truth to us. He was the first to rise again from

*literally, "the revelation *of (concerning,* or, *from)* Jesus Christ."

†literally, "in Asia."

‡literally, "the seven spirits." But see Isaiah 11:2, where various aspects of the Holy Spirit are described, and Zech. 4:26, giving probability to the paraphrase; also see chap. 2, vs. 7.

death, to die no more.* He is far greater than any king in all the earth. All praise to Him who always loves us and who set us free from our sins by pouring out His life blood for us.

6 He has gathered us into His kingdom and made us priests of God His Father. Give to Him everlasting glory! He rules forever! Amen!

7 See! He is arriving surrounded by clouds; and every eye shall see Him—yes, and those who pierced Him.† And the nations will weep in sorrow and in terror when He comes. Yes! Amen! Let it be so!

8 "I am the A and Z,‡ the Beginning and the Ending of all things," says God, who is the Lord, the All Powerful One who is, and was, and is coming again!§

9 It is I, your brother John, a fellow sufferer for the Lord's sake who is writing this letter to you. I too have shared the patience Jesus gives, and we will share His kingdom!

I was on the island of Patmos, exiled there for preaching the Word of God, and for telling what I knew about Jesus Christ.

10 It was Sunday and I was worshiping, when suddenly I heard a loud voice behind me, a voice that sounded like a trumpet blast,

11 Saying, "I am A and Z, the First and Last!" And then I heard Him say, "Write down everything

*literally, "the First-born from the dead." Others (Lazarus, etc.) rose to die again. As used here the expression therefore implies "to die no more."

†John saw this happen with his own eyes—the piercing of Jesus—and never forgot the horror of it.

‡literally, "I am Alpha and Omega"; these are the first and last letters of the Greek alphabet.

§literally, "who comes" or "who is to come."

you see, and send your letter to the seven churches
in Turkey:* to the church in Ephesus, the one in
Smyrna, and those in Pergamos, Thyatira, Sardis,
Philadelphia, and Laodicea."

12 When I turned to see who was speaking, there
behind me were seven candlesticks of gold.

13 And standing among them was One who
looked like Jesus who called himself the Son of
Man,† wearing a long robe circled with a golden
band across His chest.

14 His hair‡ was white as wool or snow, and His
eyes penetrated like flames of fire.

15 His feet gleamed like burnished bronze, and
His voice thundered like the waves against the
shore.

16 He held seven stars in His right hand and a
sharp, double-bladed sword in His mouth,§ and His
face shone like the power of the sun in unclouded
brilliance.

17, 18 When I saw Him, I fell at His feet as dead;
but He laid His right hand on me and said, "Don't
be afraid! Though I am the First and Last, the
Living One who died, who is now alive forevermore,
who has the keys of hell and death—don't be
afraid!

19 Write down what you have just seen, and
what will soon be shown to you.

20 This is the meaning of the seven stars you saw
in My right hand, and the seven golden candle-

*"The seven churches in Asia."

†literally, "like unto a Son of Man"; John recognizes Him from having lived with Him for three years, and from seeing Him in glory at the Transfiguration.

‡literally, "His head—the hair—was white like wool."

§literally, "coming out from His mouth."

sticks: The seven stars are the leaders* of the seven churches, and the seven candlesticks are the churches themselves.

CHAPTER 2

Write a letter to the leader† of the church at Ephesus and tell him this:

I write to inform you of a message from Him who walks among the churches‡ and holds their leaders in His right hand. He says to you:

2 I know how many good things you are doing. I have watched your hard work and your patience; I know you don't tolerate sin among your members, and you have carefully examined the claims of those who say they are apostles but aren't. You have found out how they lie.

3 You have patiently suffered for Me without quitting.

4 Yet there is one thing wrong: you don't love Me as at first!

5 Think about those times of your first love (how different now!) and turn back to Me again and work as you did before; or else I will come and remove your candlestick from its place among the churches.

6 But there is this about you that is good: you hate the deeds of the licentious Nicolaitanes,§ just as I do.

*literally, "angels." Some expositors (Origen, Jerome, etc.) believe from this that an angelic being is appointed by God to oversee each local church.

†literally, "angel," as in 1:20.

‡literally, "from Him who holds the seven stars in His right hand and walks among the seven golden candlesticks."

§Nicolaitanes, when translated from Greek to Hebrew, becomes Balaamites; followers of the man who induced the Israelites to fall by lust. (See Rev. 2:14 and Numbers 31:15, 16.)

7 Let this message sink into the ears of anyone who listens to what the Spirit is saying to the churches: To everyone who is victorious, I will give fruit from the Tree of Life in the Paradise of God.

* * * *

8 *To the leader* of the church in Smyrna write this letter:*

This message is from Him who is the First and Last, who was dead and then came back to life.

9 I know how much you suffer for the Lord, and I know all about your poverty (but you have heavenly riches!). I know the slander of those opposing you, who say that they are Jews—the children of God—but they aren't, for they support the cause of Satan.

10 Stop being afraid of what you are about to suffer—for the devil will soon throw some of you into prison to test you. You will be persecuted for "ten days." Become faithful even when facing death and I will give you the crown of life—an unending, glorious future.†

11 Let everyone who can hear, listen to what the Spirit is saying to the churches: he who is victorious shall not be hurt by the Second Death.

12 *Write this letter to the leader* of the church in Pergamos:*

This message is from Him who wields the sharp and double-bladed sword.

13 I am fully aware that you live in the city where Satan's throne is, at the center of Satanic worship; and yet you have remained loyal to Me,

*literally, "angel." See note on 1:20.
†implied.

and refused to deny Me, even when Antipas, My faithful witness, was martyred among you by Satan's devotees.

14 And yet I have a few things against you. You tolerate some among you who do as Balaam did when he taught Balak how to ruin the people of Israel by involving them in sexual sin, and encouraging them to go to idol feasts.

15 Yes, you have some of these very same followers of Balaam* among you!

16 Change your mind and attitude, or else I will come to you suddenly and fight against them with the sword of My mouth.

17 Let everyone who can hear, listen to what the Spirit is saying to the churches: Every one who is victorious shall eat of the hidden manna, the secret nourishment from heaven; and I will give to each a white stone, and on the stone will be engraved a new name that no one else knows except the one receiving it.

* * * *

18 *Write this letter to the leader† of the church in Thyatira:*

This is a message from the Son of God, whose eyes penetrate like flames of fire, whose feet are like glowing brass.

19 I am aware of all your good deeds—your kindness to the poor, your gifts and service to them; also I know your love and faith and patience, and I can see your constant improvement in all these things.

20 Yet I have this against you: You are permit-

*literally, "Nicolaitanes," Greek form of "Balaam."
†literally, "angel." See note on 1:20.

ting that woman Jezebel, who calls herself a prophetess, to teach My servants that sex sin is not a serious matter; she urges them to practice immorality and to eat meat that has been sacrificed to idols.

21 I gave her time to change her mind and attitude, but she refused.

22 Pay attention now to what I am saying: I will lay her upon a sickbed of intense affliction, along with all her immoral followers,* unless they turn again to Me, repenting of their sin with her;

23 And I will strike her children dead. And all the churches shall know that I am He who searches deep within men's hearts and minds; I will give to each of you whatever you deserve.

24, 25 As for the rest of you in Thyatira who have not followed this false teaching ("deeper truths," as they call them—depths of Satan, really), I will ask nothing further of you; only hold tightly to what you have until I come.

26 To every one who overcomes—who to the very end keeps on doing the things that please Me—I will give power over the nations.

27 You will rule them with a rod of iron just as My Father gave Me the authority to rule them; they will be shattered like a pot of clay that is broken into tiny pieces.

28 And I will give you the Morning Star!

29 Let all who can hear, listen to what the Spirit says to the churches.

*literally, "together with all those who commit adultery with her."

CHAPTER 3

To the leader of the church in Sardis write this letter:*

This message is sent to you by the One who has the seven-fold Spirit† of God and the seven stars.

I know your reputation as a live and active church, but you are dead.

2 Now wake up! Strengthen what little remains—for even what is left is at the point of death. Your deeds are far from right in the sight of God.

3 Go back to what you heard and believed at first; hold to it firmly and turn to Me again. Unless you do, I will come suddenly upon you, unexpected as a thief, and punish you.

4 Yet even there in Sardis some haven't soiled their garments with the world's filth; they shall walk with Me in white, for they are worthy.

5 Everyone who conquers will be clothed in white, and I will not erase his name from the Book of Life, but I will announce before My Father and His angels that he is Mine.

6 Let all who can hear, listen to what the Spirit is saying to the churches.

* * * *

7 *Write this letter to the leader* of the church in Philadelphia:*

This message is sent to you by the One who is holy and true, and has the key of David to open what no one can shut and to shut what no one can open.

*literally, "angel." See note on 1:20.
†literally, "the seven spirits of God." See note on 1:4.

8 I know you well: you aren't strong, but you have tried to obey* and have not denied My Name: Therefore I have opened a door to you that no one can shut.

9 Note this: I will force those supporting the causes of Satan while claiming to be Mine† (but they aren't—they are lying) to fall at your feet and acknowledge that you are the ones I love.

10 Because you have patiently obeyed Me despite the persecution, therefore I will protect you from‡ the time of Great Tribulation and temptation, which will come upon the world to test everyone alive.

11 Look, I am coming soon!§ Hold tightly to the little strength you have—so that no one will take away your crown.

12 As for the one who conquers, I will make him a pillar in the temple of My God; he will be secure, and will go out no more; and I will write My God's Name on him, and he will be a citizen in the city of My God—the New Jerusalem, coming down from heaven from My God; and he will have My new Name inscribed upon him.

13 Let all who can hear, listen to what the Spirit is saying to the churches.

* * * *

14 *Write this letter to the leader** of the church in Laodicea:*

*literally, "you have kept My word."

†literally, "say they are Jews but are not."

‡or, "I will keep you from failing in the hour of testing . . ." The inference is not clear in the Greek as to whether this means "kept from" or "kept through" the coming horror.

§or, "suddenly," "unexpectedly."

**literally, "angel." See note on 1:20.

This message is from the One who stands firm,* the faithful and true Witness (of all that is or was or evermore shall be),† the primeval source of God's creation:

15 I know you well—you are neither hot nor cold; I wish you were one or the other!

16 But since you are merely lukewarm, I will spit you out of My mouth!

17 You say, "I am rich, with everything I want; I don't need a thing!" And you don't realize that spiritually you are wretched and miserable and poor and blind and naked.

18 My advice to you is to buy pure gold from Me, gold purified by fire—only then will you truly be rich. And to purchase from Me white garments, clean and pure, so you won't be naked and ashamed; and to get medicine from Me to heal your eyes and give you back your sight.

19 I continually discipline and punish everyone I love; so I must punish you, unless you turn from your indifference and become enthusiastic about the things of God.

20 Look! I have been standing at the door and I am constantly knocking. If anyone hears Me calling him and opens the door, I will come in and fellowship with him and he with Me.

21 I will let every one who conquers sit beside Me on My throne, just as I took My place with My Father on His throne when I had conquered.

22 Let those who can hear, listen to what the Spirit is saying to the churches.

*literally, "from the Amen."
†implied. Literally, "the faithful and true witness."

CHAPTER 4

Then as I looked, I saw a door standing open in heaven, and the same voice I had heard before, that sounded like a mighty trumpet blast, spoke to me and said,

"Come up here and I will show you what must happen in the future!"

2 And instantly I was, in spirit, there in heaven and saw—oh the glory of it!—a throne and someone sitting on it!

3 Great bursts of light flashed forth from Him as from a glittering diamond, or from a shining ruby, and a rainbow glowing like an emerald encircled His throne.

4 Twenty-four smaller thrones surrounded His, with twenty-four elders sitting on them; all were clothed in white, with golden crowns upon their heads.

5 Lightning and thunder issued from the throne, and there were voices in the thunder. Directly in front of His throne were seven lighted lamps representing the seven-fold Spirit* of God.

6 Spread out before it was a shiny crystal sea. Four Living Beings, dotted front and back with eyes, stood at the throne's four sides.

7 The first of these Living Beings was in the form of a lion; the second looked like an ox; the third had the face of a man; and the fourth, the form of an eagle, with wings spread out as though in flight.

*literally, "the seven spirits of God." But see Zech. 4:2-6, where the lamps are equated with the one Spirit.

8 Each of these Living Beings had six wings, and the central sections of their wings were covered with eyes. Day after day and night after night they kept on saying, "Holy, holy, holy, Lord God Almighty—the One who was, and is, and is to come."

9 And when the Living Beings give glory and honor and thanks to the One sitting on the throne, who lives forever and ever,

10 The twenty-four elders fall down before Him and worship Him, the Eternal Living One, and cast their crowns before the throne, singing,

11 "Oh Lord, You are worthy to receive the glory and the honor and the power, for You have created all things. They were created and called into being by Your act of will."

CHAPTER 5

And I saw a scroll in the right hand of the One who was sitting on the throne, a scroll with writing on the inside and on the back, and sealed with seven seals.

2 A mighty angel with a loud voice was shouting out this question: "Who is worthy to break the seals on this scroll, and to unroll it?"

3 But no one in all heaven or earth or from among the dead was permitted to open and read it.

4 Then I wept with disappointment* because no one anywhere was worthy; no one could tell us what it said.

5 But one of the twenty-four elders said to me,

*implied.

"Cease weeping, for look! The Lion of the tribe of Judah, the Root of David, has conquered, and proved Himself worthy to open the scroll and to break its seven seals."

6 I looked and saw a Lamb standing there before the twenty-four elders, in front of the throne and the Living Beings, and on the Lamb were wounds that once had caused His death. He had seven horns and seven eyes, which represent the sevenfold Spirit* of God, sent out into every part of the world.

7 He stepped forward and took the scroll from the right hand of the One sitting upon the throne.

8 And as He took the scroll, the twenty-four elders fell down before the Lamb, each with a harp and golden vials filled with incense—the prayers of God's people!

9 They were singing Him a new song with these words: "You are worthy to take the scroll and break its seals and open it; for You were slain, and Your blood has bought people from every nation as gifts for God.

10 And You have gathered them into a kingdom and made them priests of our God; they shall reign upon the earth."

11 Then in my vision I heard the singing of millions of angels surrounding the throne and the Living Beings and the elders:

12 "The Lamb is worthy" (loudly they sang it!) "—the Lamb who was slain. He is worthy to re-

*literally, "the seven spirits of God"; but see Zechariah 4:2-6, 10, where the seven eyes are equated with the seven lamps and the one Spirit.

ceive the power, and the riches, and the wisdom,
and the strength, and the honor, and the glory, and
the blessing."
13 And then I heard everyone in heaven and
earth, and from the dead beneath the earth and in
the sea, exclaiming, "The blessing and the honor
and the glory and the power belong to the One sitting on the throne, and to the Lamb forever and
ever."
14 And the four Living Beings kept saying,
"Amen!" And the twenty-four elders fell down and
worshiped Him.

CHAPTER 6

As I watched, the Lamb broke the first seal and
began to unroll the scroll. Then one of the four
Living Beings, with a voice that sounded like thunder, said, "Come!"
2 I looked, and there in front of me was a white
horse. Its rider carried a bow, and a crown was
placed upon his head; he rode out to conquer in
many battles and win the war.
3 Then He unrolled the scroll to the second seal,
and broke it open, too. And I heard the second
Living Being say, "Come!"
4 This time a red horse rode out. Its rider was
given a long sword and the authority to banish
peace and bring anarchy to the earth; war and killing broke out everywhere.
5 When He had broken the third seal, I heard
the third Living Being say, "Come!" And I saw a
black horse, with its rider holding a pair of balances
in his hand.

[6] And a voice from among the four Living Beings said, "A loaf of bread for a dollar, or three pounds of barley flour,* but there is no olive oil or wine."†

[7] And when the fourth seal was broken, I heard the fourth Living Being say, "Come!"

[8] And now I saw a pale horse, and its rider's name was Death. And there followed after him another horse whose rider's name was Hell. They were given control of one-fourth of the earth, to kill with war and famine and disease and wild animals.

[9] And when He broke open the fifth seal, I saw an altar, and underneath it all the souls of those who had been martyred for preaching the Word of God and for being faithful in their witnessing.

[10] They called loudly to the Lord and said, "Oh Sovereign Lord, holy and true, how long will it be before You judge the people of the earth for what they've done to us? When will You avenge our blood against those living on the earth?"

[11] White robes were given to each of them, and they were told to rest a little longer until their other brothers, fellow servants of Jesus, had been martyred on the earth and joined them.

[12] I watched as He broke the sixth seal, and there was a vast earthquake; and the sun became dark like black cloth, and the moon was blood-red.

*literally, "A choenix of wheat for a denarius, and three choenix of barley for a denarius. . . ."

†literally, "do not damage the oil and wine."

13 Then the stars of heaven appeared to be falling to earth*—like green fruit from fig trees buffeted by mighty winds.

14 And the starry heavens disappeared† as though rolled up like a scroll and taken away; and every mountain and island shook and shifted.

15 The kings of the earth, and world leaders and rich men, and high-ranking military officers, and all men great and small, slave and free, hid themselves in the caves and rocks of the mountains,

16 And cried to the mountains to crush them. "Fall on us," they pleaded, "and hide us from the face of the One sitting on the throne, and from the anger of the Lamb,

17 Because the great day of their anger has come, and who can survive it?"

CHAPTER 7

Then I saw four angels standing at the four corners of the earth, holding back the four winds from blowing, so that not a leaf rustled in the trees, and the ocean became as smooth as glass.

2 And I saw another angel coming from the east, carrying the Great Seal of the Living God. And he shouted out to those four angels who had been given power to injure earth and sea,

3 "Wait! Don't do anything yet—hurt neither earth nor sea nor trees—until we have placed the Seal of God upon the foreheads of His servants."

*literally, "the stars of heaven fell to the earth."
†literally, "the sky departed."

4 How many were given this mark? I heard the number—it was 144,000, out of all twelve tribes of Israel, as listed here:

5	Judah	12,000
	Reuben	12,000
	Gad	12,000
6	Asher	12,000
	Naphtali	12,000
	Manasseh	12,000
7	Simeon	12,000
	Levi	12,000
	Issachar	12,000
8	Zebulun	12,000
	Joseph	12,000
	Benjamin	12,000

9 After this I saw a vast crowd, too great to count, from all nations and provinces and languages, standing in front of the throne and before the Lamb, clothed in white, with palm branches in their hands.

10 And they were shouting with a mighty shout, "Salvation comes from our God upon the throne, and from the Lamb."

11 And now all the angels were crowding around the throne and around the elders and the four Living Beings, and falling face down before the throne and worshiping God.

12 "Amen!" they said. "Blessing, and glory, and wisdom, and thanksgiving, and honor, and power, and might be to our God forever and forever. Amen!"

13 Then one of the twenty-four elders asked me,

"Do you know who these are, who are clothed in white, and where they come from?"

14 "No, sir," I replied. "Please tell me."

"These are the ones coming out of the Great Tribulation," he said; "they washed their robes and whitened them by the blood of the Lamb.

15 That is why they are here before the throne of God, serving Him day and night in His temple. The One sitting on the throne will shelter them;

16 They will never be hungry again, nor thirsty, and they will be fully protected from the scorching noontime heat.

17 For the Lamb standing in front of* the throne will feed them and be their Shepherd and lead them to the springs of the Water of Life. And God will wipe their tears away."

CHAPTER 8

When the Lamb had broken the seventh seal, there was silence throughout all heaven for what seemed like half an hour.

2 And I saw the seven angels that stand before God, and they were given seven trumpets.

3 Then another angel with a golden censer came and stood at the altar; and a great quantity of incense was given to him to mix with the prayers of God's people, to offer upon the golden altar before the throne.

4 And the perfume of the incense mixed with

*literally, "in the center of the throne"; i.e., directly in front, not to one side. An alternate rendering might be, "at the heart of the throne."

prayers ascended up to God from the altar where
the angel had poured them out.

5 Then the angel filled the censer with fire from
the altar and threw it down upon the earth; and
thunder crashed and rumbled, lightning flashed,
and there was a terrible earthquake.

6 Then the seven angels with the seven trumpets
prepared to blow their mighty blasts.

7 The first angel blew his trumpet, and hail and
fire mixed with blood were thrown down upon the
earth. One-third of the earth was set on fire so
that one-third of the trees were burned, and all
the green grass.

8, 9 Then the second angel blew his trumpet, and
what appeared to be a huge burning mountain was
thrown into the sea, destroying a third of all the
ships; and a third of the sea turned red as* blood;
and a third of the fish were killed.

10 The third angel blew, and a great flaming star
fell from heaven upon a third of the rivers and
springs.

11 The star was called "Bitterness"† because it
poisoned a third of all the water on the earth and
many people died.

12 The fourth angel blew his trumpet and immediately a third of the sun was blighted and
darkened, and a third of the moon and the stars,
so that the daylight was dimmed by a third, and
the nighttime darkness deepened.

13 As I watched, I saw a solitary eagle flying
through the heavens crying loudly, "Woe, woe, woe

*literally, "became blood."
†literally, "wormwood."

to the people of the earth because of the terrible things that will soon happen when the three remaining angels blow their trumpets."

CHAPTER 9

Then the fifth angel blew his trumpet and I saw one* who was fallen to earth from heaven, and to him was given the key to the bottomless pit.

2 When he opened it, smoke poured out as though from some huge furnace, and the sun and air were darkened by the smoke.

3 Then locusts came from the smoke and descended onto the earth and were given power to sting like scorpions.

4 They were told not to hurt the grass or plants or trees, but to attack those people who did not have the mark of God on their foreheads.

5 They were not to kill them, but to torture them for five months with agony like the pain of scorpion stings.

6 In those days men will try to kill themselves but won't be able to—death will not come. They will long to die—but death will flee away!

7 The locusts looked like horses armored for battle. They had what looked like golden crowns on their heads, and their faces looked like men's.

*literally, "a star fallen from heaven." It is unclear whether this person is of Satanic origin, as most commentators believe, or whether the reference is to Christ.

8 Their hair was long like women's, and their teeth were those of lions.

9 They wore breastplates that seemed to be of iron, and their wings roared like an army of chariots rushing into battle.

10 They had stinging tails like scorpions, and their power to hurt, given to them for five months, was in their tails.

11 Their king is the Prince of the bottomless pit whose name in Hebrew is Abaddon, and in Greek, Apollyon, (and in English, the Destroyer).*

12 One terror now ends, but there are two more coming!

13 The sixth angel blew his trumpet and I heard a voice speaking from the four horns of the golden altar that stands before the throne of God,

14 Saying to the sixth angel, "Release the four mighty demons† held bound at the great River Euphrates."

15 They had been kept in readiness for that year and month and day and hour, and now they were turned loose to kill a third of all mankind.

16 They led an army of 200,000,000‡ warriors§—I heard an announcement of how many there were.

17, 18 I saw their horses spread out before me in my vision; their riders wore fiery-red breastplates, though some were sky-blue and others yellow. The horses' heads looked much like lions', and smoke

*implied.

†literally, "(fallen) angels."

‡If this is a literal figure, it is no longer incredible, in view of a world population of 6,000 million in the near future. In China alone, in 1961, there were "an estimated 200,000,000 armed and organized militiamen" (Associated Press release, April 24, 1964).

§literally, "horsemen."

and fire and flaming sulphur bellowed from their
mouths, killing one-third of all mankind.

19 Their power of death was not only in their
mouths, but in their tails as well, for their tails
were similar to serpents' heads that struck and bit
with fatal wounds.

20 But the men left alive after these plagues *still
refused to worship God!* They would not renounce
their demon-worship, nor their idols made of gold
and silver, brass, stone, and wood—which neither
see nor hear nor walk!

21 Neither did they change their mind and attitude about all their murders and witchcraft, their
immorality and theft.

CHAPTER 10

Then I saw another mighty angel coming down
from heaven, surrounded by a cloud, with a rainbow over his head; his face shone like the sun and
his feet flashed with fire.

2 And he held open in his hand a small scroll.
He set his right foot on the sea and his left foot on
the earth,

3 And gave a great shout—it was like the
roar of a lion—and the seven thunders crashed their
reply.

4 I was about to write what the thunders said
when a voice from heaven called to me, "Don't do
it. Their words are not to be revealed."

5 Then the mighty angel standing on the sea and
land lifted his right hand to heaven,

6 And swore by Him who lives forever and ever,
who created heaven and everything in it and the
earth and all that it contains and the sea and its
inhabitants, that there should be no more delay,

7 But that when the seventh angel blows his
trumpet, then God's veiled plan—mysterious
through the ages ever since it was announced by
His servants the prophets—will be fulfilled.

8 Then the voice from heaven spoke to me again,
"Go and get the unrolled scroll from the mighty
angel standing there upon the sea and land."

9 So I approached him and asked him to give
me the scroll. "Yes, take it and eat it," he said.
"At first it will taste like honey, but when you
swallow it, it will make your stomach sour!"

10 So I took it from his hand, and ate it! and just
as he had said, it was sweet in my mouth but it
gave me a stomach-ache when I swallowed it.

11 Then he told me, "You must prophesy further
about many peoples, nations, tribes and kings."

CHAPTER 11

Now I was given a measuring stick and told to
go and measure the temple of God, including the
inner court where the altar stands, and to count
the number of worshipers.*

2 "But do not measure the outer court," I was

*literally, "Rise and measure the temple of God, and the altar, and them that worship therein."

told, "for it has been turned over to the nations.
They will trample over the Holy City for forty-two
months.*

3 And I will give power to My two witnesses to
prophesy 1260 days* clothed in sackcloth."

4 These two prophets are the two olive trees,†
and two candlesticks standing before the God of
all the earth.

5 Anyone trying to harm them will be killed by
bursts of fire shooting from their mouths.

6 They have power to shut the skies so that no
rain will fall during the three and a half years they
prophesy, and to turn rivers and oceans to blood,
and to send every kind of plague upon the earth as
often as they wish.

7 When they complete the three and a half years
of their solemn testimony, the tyrant who comes
out of the bottomless pit‡ will declare war against
them and conquer and kill them;

8, 9 And for three and a half days their bodies
will be exposed in the streets of Jerusalem (the city
fittingly described as "Sodom" or "Egypt")—the
very place where their Lord was crucified. No one
will be allowed to bury them, and people from many
nations will crowd around to gaze at them.

10 And there will be a worldwide holiday—people
everywhere will rejoice and give presents to each
other and throw parties to celebrate the death of
the two prophets who had tormented them so
much!

11 But after three and a half days, the spirit of

*3½ years, as in Daniel 12:7.
†Zechariah 4:3, 4, 11.
‡Revelation 9:11.

life from God will enter them and they will stand
up! And great fear will fall on everyone.

12 Then a loud voice will shout from heaven,
"Come up!" And they will rise to heaven in a cloud
as their enemies watch.

13 The same hour there will be a terrible earthquake that levels a tenth of the city leaving 7000
dead. Then everyone left will, in their terror, give
glory to the God of heaven.

14 The second woe is past, but the third quickly
follows:

15 For just then the seventh angel blew his trumpet, and there were loud voices shouting down
from heaven, "The kingdom of this world now belongs to our Lord, and to His Christ; and He shall
reign forever and ever."*

16 And the twenty-four elders sitting on their
thrones before God threw themselves down in worship, saying,

17 "We give thanks, Lord God Almighty, who
is and was, for now You have assumed Your great
power and have begun to reign.

18 The nations were angry with You, but now
it is Your turn to be angry with them. It is time to
judge the dead, and reward Your servants—prophets and people alike, all who fear Your Name, both
great and small—and to destroy those who have
caused destruction upon the earth."

*or, "The Lord and His Anointed shall now rule the world from this day to eternity."

[19] Then, in heaven, the temple of God was opened and the ark of His covenant could be seen inside. Lightning flashed and thunder crashed and roared, and there was a great hailstorm and the world was shaken by a mighty earthquake.

CHAPTER 12

Then a great pageant appeared in heaven, portraying things to come. I saw a woman clothed with the sun, with the moon beneath her feet, and a crown of twelve stars on her head.

[2] She was pregnant and screamed in the pain of her labor, awaiting her delivery.

[3] Suddenly a red Dragon appeared, with seven heads and ten horns, and seven crowns on his heads.

[4] His tail drew along behind him a third of the stars, which he plunged to the earth. He stood before the woman as she was about to give birth to her child, ready to eat the baby as soon as it was born.

[5] She gave birth to a boy who was to rule all nations with a heavy hand, and He was caught up to God and to His throne.

[6] The woman fled into the wilderness, where God had prepared a place for her, to take care of her for 1260 days.

[7] Then there was war in heaven; Michael and the angels under his command fought the Dragon and his hosts of fallen angels.

[8] And the Dragon lost the battle and was forced from heaven.

9 This great Dragon—the ancient serpent called the Devil, or Satan, the one deceiving the whole world—was thrown down onto the earth with all his army.

10 Then I heard a loud voice shouting across the heavens, "It has happened at last! God's salvation and the power and the rule, and the authority of His Christ are finally here; for the Accuser of our brothers has been thrown down from heaven onto earth—he accused them day and night before our God.

11 They defeated him by the blood of the Lamb, and by their testimony; for they did not love their lives but laid them down for Him.

12 Rejoice, oh heavens! you citizens of heaven, rejoice! be glad! But woe to you people of the world, for the Devil has come down to you in great anger, knowing that he has little time."

13 And when the Dragon found himself cast down to earth, he persecuted the woman who had given birth to the child.

14 But she was given two wings like those of a great eagle, to fly into the wilderness to the place prepared for her, where she was cared for and protected from the Serpent, the Dragon, for three and a half years.*

15 And from the Serpent's mouth a vast flood of water gushed out and swept toward the woman in an effort to get rid of her;

16 But the earth helped her by opening its mouth and swallowing the flood!

17 Then the furious Dragon set out to attack the rest of her children—all who were keeping God's

*literally, "a time and times and half a time."

commandments and confessing that they belong to Jesus. He stood waiting on an ocean beach.

CHAPTER 13

And now, in my vision, I saw a strange Creature rising up out of the sea. It had seven heads and ten horns, and ten crowns upon its horns. And written on each head were blasphemous names, each one defying and insulting God.

2 This Creature looked like a leopard but had bear's feet and a lion's mouth! And the Dragon gave him his own power and throne and great authority.

3 I saw that one of his heads seemed wounded beyond recovery—but the fatal wound was healed! All the world marveled at this miracle and followed the Creature in awe.

4 They worshiped the Dragon for giving him such power, and they worshiped the strange Creature. "Where is there anyone as great as he?" they exclaimed. "Who is able to fight against him?"

5 Then the Dragon encouraged the Creature to speak great blasphemies against the Lord; and gave him authority to control the earth for forty-two months.

6 All that time he blasphemed God's name and His temple and all those living in heaven.

7 The Dragon gave him power to fight against God's people* and to overcome them, and to rule over all nations and language groups throughout the world.

8 And all mankind—whose names were not writ-

*literally, "It was permitted to fight against God's people."

ten down before the founding of the world in the slain* Lamb's Book of Life—worshiped the evil Creature.

9 Anyone who can hear, listen carefully:

10 The people of God who are destined for prison will be arrested and taken away; those destined for death will be killed.† But do not be dismayed, for here is your opportunity for endurance and confidence.

11 Then I saw another strange animal, this one coming up out of the earth, with two little horns like those of a lamb but a fearsome voice like the Dragon's.

12 He exercised all the authority of the Creature whose death-wound had been healed, whom he required all the world to worship.

13 He did unbelievable miracles such as making fire flame down to earth from the skies while everyone was watching.

14 By doing these miracles, he was deceiving people everywhere. He could do these marvelous things whenever the first Creature was there to watch him. And he ordered the people of the world to make a great statue of the first Creature, who was fatally wounded and then came back to life.

15 He was permitted to give breath to this statue and even make it speak! Then the statue ordered that anyone refusing to worship it must die!

16 He required everyone—great and small, rich

*or, "those whose names were not written in the Book of Life of the Lamb slain before the founding of the world." That is, regarded as slain in the eternal plan of and knowledge of God.

†or, "If anyone imprisons you, he will be imprisoned! If anyone kills you, he will be killed!"

and poor, slave and free—to be tattooed with a certain mark on the right hand or on the forehead.

17 And no one could get a job or even buy in any store without the permit of that mark, which was either the name of the creature or the code number of his name.

18 Here is a puzzle that calls for careful thought to solve it. Let those who are able, interpret this code: the numerical values of the letters in his name add to 666!*

CHAPTER 14

Then I saw a Lamb standing on Mount Zion in Jerusalem, and with Him were 144,000 who had His Name and His Father's Name written on their foreheads.

2 And I heard a sound from heaven like the roaring of a great waterfall or the rolling of mighty thunder. It was the singing of a choir accompanied by harps.

3 This tremendous choir—144,000 strong—sang a wonderful new song in front of the throne of God, and before the four Living Beings and the twenty-four elders; and no one could sing this song except these 144,000 who had been redeemed from the earth.

4 For they are spiritually undefiled, pure as virgins,† following the Lamb wherever He goes. They have been purchased from among the men on the earth as a consecrated offering to God and the Lamb.

*Some manuscripts read "616."
†literally, "They have not defiled themselves with women, for they are virgins."

5 No falsehood can be charged against them; they are blameless.

6 And I saw another angel flying through the heavens, carrying the everlasting Good News to preach to those on earth—to every nation, tribe, language and people.

7 "Fear God," he shouted, "and extol His greatness. For the time has come when He will sit as Judge. Worship Him who made the heaven and the earth, the sea and all its sources."

8 Then another angel followed him through the skies, saying, "Babylon is fallen, is fallen—that great city—because she seduced the nations of the world and made them share the wine of her intense impurity and sin."

9 Then a third angel followed them shouting, "Anyone worshiping the Creature from the sea* and his statue and accepting his mark on the forehead or the hand,

10 Must drink the wine of the anger of God; it is poured out undiluted into God's cup of wrath. And they will be tormented with fire and burning sulphur in the presence of the holy angels and the Lamb.

11 The smoke of their torture rises forever and ever, and they will have no relief day or night, for they have worshiped the Creature and his statue, and have been tattooed with the code of his name.

12 Let this encourage God's people to endure patiently every trial and persecution, for they are

*implied.

His saints who remain firm to the end in obedience to His commands and trust in Jesus."

13 And I heard a voice in the heavens above me saying, "Write this down: At last the time has come for His martyrs* to enter into their full reward. Yes, says the Spirit, they are blest indeed, for now they shall rest from all their toils and trials; for their good deeds follow them to heaven!"

14 Then the scene changed and I saw a white cloud, and Someone sitting on it who looked like Jesus, who was called "The Son of Man,"† with a crown of solid gold upon His head and a sharp sickle in His hand.

15 Then an angel came from the temple and called out to Him, "Begin to use the sickle, for the time has come for You to reap; the harvest is ripe on the earth."

16 So the One sitting on the cloud swung His sickle over the earth, and the harvest was gathered in.

17 After that another angel came from the temple in heaven, and he also had a sharp sickle.

18 Just then the angel who has power to destroy the world with fire,‡ shouted to the angel with the sickle, "Use your sickle now to cut off the clusters of grapes from the vines of the earth, for they are fully ripe for judgment."

19 So the angel swung his sickle on the earth and loaded the grapes into the great winepress of God's wrath.

*literally, "those who die in the faith of Jesus." Verse 12 implies death from persecution for Christ's sake.

†literally, "one like a Son of man."

‡literally, "who has power over fire."

20 And the grapes were trodden in the winepress
outside the city, and blood flowed out in a stream
200 miles long and as high as a horse's bridle.

CHAPTER 15

And I saw in heaven another mighty pageant showing things to come: seven angels were assigned to carry down to earth the seven last plagues—and then at last God's anger will be finished.

2 Spread out before me was what seemed to be
an ocean of fire and glass, and on it stood all those
who had been victorious over the Evil Creature and
his statue and his mark and number. All were holding harps of God,

3 And they were singing the song of Moses, the
servant of God, and the song of the Lamb:

"Great and marvelous
Are Your doings,
Lord God Almighty.
Just and true
Are Your ways,
Oh King of Ages*

4 Who shall not fear,
Oh Lord,
And glorify Your Name?
For You alone are holy.
All nations will come
And worship before You,
For Your righteous deeds
Have been disclosed."

*Some manuscripts read, "King of the Nations."

5 Then I looked and saw that the Holy of Holies
of the temple in heaven was thrown wide open!

6 The seven angels who were assigned to pour
out the seven plagues then came from the temple,
clothed in spotlessly white linen, with golden belts
across their chests.

7 And one of the four Living Beings handed each
of them a golden flask filled with the terrible wrath
of the Living God who lives forever and forever.

8 The temple was filled with smoke from His
glory and power; and no one could enter until the
seven angels had completed pouring out the seven
plagues.

CHAPTER 16

And I heard a mighty voice shouting from the
temple to the seven angels, "Now go your ways
and empty out the seven flasks of the wrath of God
upon the earth."

2 So the first angel left the temple and poured
out his flask over the earth, and horrible, malignant
sores broke out on everyone who had the mark of
the Creature and was worshiping his statue.

3 The second angel poured out his flask upon the
oceans, and they become like the watery blood of a
dead man; and everything in all the oceans died.

4 The third angel poured out his flask upon the
rivers and springs and they became blood.

5 And I heard this angel of the waters declaring,
"You are just in sending this judgment, oh Holy
One, who is and was,

6 For Your saints and prophets have been martyred and their blood poured out upon the earth;
and now, in turn, You have poured out the blood
of those who murdered them; it is their just reward."

7 And I heard the angel of the altar* say, "Yes,
Lord God Almighty, Your punishments are just
and true."

8 Then the fourth angel poured out his flask
upon the sun, causing it to scorch all men with its
fire.

9 Everyone was burned by this blast of heat, and
they cursed the name of God who sent the plagues
—they did not change their mind and attitude to
give Him glory.

10 Then the fifth angel poured out his flask upon
the throne of the Creature from the sea,† and his
kingdom was plunged into darkness. And his sub-
jects gnawed their tongues in anguish,

11 And cursed the God of heaven for their pains
and sores, but they refused to repent of all their
evil deeds.

12 The sixth angel poured out his flask upon the
great River Euphrates and it dried up so that the
kings from the east could march their armies west-
ward without hindrance.

13 And I saw three evil spirits disguised as frogs
leap from the mouth of the Dragon, the Creature,
and his False Prophet.‡

*literally, "I heard the altar cry. . . ."
†implied.
‡Described in Chap. 13:11-15 and 19:20.

[14] These miracle-working demons conferred with all the rulers of the world to gather them for battle against the Lord on that great coming Judgment Day of God Almighty.

[15] "Take note: I will come as unexpectedly as a thief! Blessed are all who are awaiting Me, who keep their robes in readiness and will not need to walk naked and ashamed."

[16] And they gathered all the armies of the world near a place called, in Hebrew, Armageddon—the Mountain of Megiddo.

[17] Then the seventh angel poured out his flask into the air; and a mighty shout came from the throne of the temple in heaven, saying, "It is finished!"*

[18] Then the thunder crashed and rolled, and lightning flashed; and there was a great earthquake of a magnitude unprecedented in human history.

[19] The great city of "Babylon" split into three sections, and cities around the world fell in heaps of rubble; and so all of "Babylon's" sins were remembered in God's thoughts, and she was punished to the last drop of anger in the cup of the wine of the fierceness of His wrath.

[20] And islands vanished, and mountains flattened out,

[21] And there was an incredible hailstorm from heaven; hailstones weighing a hundred pounds fell from the sky onto the people below, and they cursed God because of the terrible hail.

***literally, "it has happened." An epoch of human history has come to an end.**

CHAPTER 17

One of the seven angels who had poured out the plagues came over and talked with me. "Come with me," he said, "and I will show you what is going to happen to the Notorious Prostitute, who sits upon the many waters of the world.

2 The kings of the world have had immoral relations with her, and the people of the earth have been made drunk by the wine of her immorality."

3 So the angel took me in spirit into the wilderness. There I saw a woman sitting on a scarlet animal that had seven heads and ten horns,* written all over with blasphemies against God.

4 The woman wore purple and scarlet clothing and beautiful jewelry made of gold and precious gems and pearls, and held in her hand a golden goblet full of obscenities.

5 A mysterious caption was written on her forehead: "Babylon the Great, Mother of Prostitutes and of Idol Worship Everywhere around the World."

6 I could see that she was drunk—drunk with the blood of the martyrs of Jesus she had killed. I stared at her in horror.

7 "Why are you so surprised?" the angel asked. "I'll tell you who she is and what the animal she is riding represents.

8 He was alive but isn't now. And yet, soon, he

*As the Dragon—Satan—and the Creature from the sea are also described in 12:3, 9 and 13:1.

will come up out of the bottomless pit and go to eternal destruction;* and the people of earth, whose names have not been written in the Book of Life before the world began, will be dumbfounded at his reappearance after being dead.†

9 And now think hard: His seven heads represent a certain city‡ built on seven hills where this woman has her residence.

10 They also represent seven kings. Five have already fallen, the sixth now reigns, and the seventh is yet to come, but his reign will be brief.

11 The scarlet animal that died is the eighth king, having reigned before as one of the seven; after his second reign, he too will go to his doom.*

12 His ten horns are ten kings who have not yet risen to power; they will be appointed to their kingdoms for one brief moment, to reign with him.

13 They will all sign a treaty giving their power and strength to him.

14 Together they will wage war against the Lamb, and the Lamb will conquer them; for He is Lord over all lords, and King of kings, and His people are the called and chosen and faithful ones.

15 The oceans, lakes and rivers that the woman is sitting on represent masses of people of every race and nation.

16 The scarlet animal and his ten horns—which represent ten kings who will reign with him—all

*literally, "go to perdition."
†literally, "dumbfounded at the ruler who was, and is not, and will be present."
‡implied from verse 18.

hate the woman, and will attack her and leave her naked and ravaged by fire.

17 For God will put a plan into their minds, a plan that will carry out His purposes: they will mutually agree to give their authority to the scarlet animal, so that the words of God will be fulfilled.

18 And this woman you saw in your vision represents the great city that rules over the kings of the earth."

CHAPTER 18

After all this I saw another angel come down from heaven with great authority, and the earth grew bright with his splendor.

2 He gave a mighty shout, "Babylon the Great is fallen, is fallen; she has become a den of demons, a haunt of devils and every kind of evil spirit.*

3 For all the nations have drunk the fatal wine of her intense immorality. The rulers of the earth have enjoyed themselves† with her, and businessmen throughout the world have grown rich from all her luxurious living."

4 Then I heard another voice calling from heaven, "Come away from her, My people; do not take part in her sins, or you will be punished with her.

5 For her sins are piled as high as heaven and God is ready to judge her for her crimes.

6 Do to her as she has done to you, and more—

*literally, "of every foul and hateful bird."
†literally, "have committed fornication with her."

give double penalty for all her evil deeds. She brewed many a cup of woe for others—give twice as much to her.

7 She has lived in luxury and pleasure—match it now with torments and with sorrows. She boasts, 'I am queen upon my throne. I am no helpless widow. I will not experience sorrow.'

8 Therefore the sorrows of death and mourning and famine shall overtake her in a single day, and she shall be utterly consumed by fire; for mighty is the Lord who judges her."

9 And the world leaders, who took part in her immoral acts and enjoyed her favors, will mourn for her as they see the smoke rising from her charred remains.

10 They will stand far off trembling with fear and crying out, "Alas, Babylon, that mighty city! In one moment her judgment fell."

11 The merchants of the earth will weep and mourn for her, for there is no one left to buy their goods.

12 She was their biggest customer for gold and silver, precious stones, pearls, finest linens, purple silks, and scarlet; and every kind of perfumed wood, and ivory goods and most expensive wooden carvings, and brass and iron and marble;

13 And spices and perfumes and incense, ointment and frankincense, wine, olive oil, and fine flour; wheat, cattle, sheep, horses, chariots, and slaves—and even the souls of men.

14 "All the fancy things you loved so much are gone," they cry, "the dainty luxuries and splendor that you prized so much will never be yours again. They are gone forever."

15 And so the merchants who have become
wealthy by selling her these things shall stand at a
distance, fearing danger to themselves, weeping and
crying.

16 "Alas, that great city, so beautiful—like a
woman clothed in finest purple and scarlet linens,
decked out with gold and precious stones and
pearls!

17 In one moment, all the wealth of the city is
gone!" And all the shipowners and captains of the
merchant ships and crews will stand a long way off,

18 Crying as they watch the smoke ascend and
saying, "Where in all the world is there another
city such as this?"

19 And they will throw dust on their heads in
their sorrow and say, "Alas, alas, for that great
city! She made us all rich from her great wealth.
And now in a single hour all is gone. . . ."

20 But you, oh heaven, rejoice over her fate; and
you, oh children of God and the prophets and the
apostles! For at last God has given judgment
against her for you.

21 Then a mighty angel picked up a boulder
shaped like a millstone and threw it into the ocean
and shouted, "Babylon, that great city, shall be
thrown away as I have thrown away this stone, and
she shall disappear forever.

22 Never again will the sound of music be there—
no more pianos, saxophones, and trumpets.* No in-
dustry of any kind will ever again exist there, and
there will be no more milling of the grain.

*literally, "harpers . . . pipers . . . and trumpeters."

23 Dark, dark will be her nights; not even a lamp in a window will ever be seen again. No more joyous wedding bells and happy voices of the bridegrooms and the brides. Her businessmen were known around the world and she deceived all nations with her sorceries.

24 And she was responsible for the blood of all the martyred prophets and the saints."

CHAPTER 19

After this I heard the shouting of a vast crowd in heaven, "Hallelujah! Praise the Lord! Salvation is from our God. Honor and authority belong to Him alone;

2 For His judgments are just and true. He has punished the Great Prostitute who corrupted the earth with her sin;* and He has avenged the murder of His servants."

3 Again and again their voices rang, "Praise the Lord! The smoke from her burning ascends forever and forever!"

4 Then the twenty-four elders and four Living Beings fell down and worshiped God, who was sitting upon the throne, and said, "Amen! Hallelujah! Praise the Lord!"

5 And out of the throne came a voice that said, "Praise our God, all you His servants, small and great, who fear Him."

6 Then I heard again what sounded like the

*literally, "fornication," the word used symbolically through the prophets for the worship of false gods.

shouting of a huge crowd, or like the waves of a hundred oceans crashing on the shore, or like the mighty rolling of great thunder, "Praise the Lord. For the Lord our God, the Almighty, reigns.

7 Let us be glad and rejoice and honor Him; for the time has come for the wedding banquet of the Lamb, and His bride has prepared herself.

8 She is permitted to wear the cleanest and whitest and finest of linens." (Fine linen represents the good deeds done by the people of God.)

9 And the angel* dictated this sentence to me: "Blessed are those who are invited to the wedding feast of the Lamb." And he added, "God Himself has stated this."†

10 Then I fell down at his feet to worship him, but he said, "No! Don't! For I am a servant of God just as you are, and as your brother Christians are, who testify of their faith in Jesus. The purpose of all prophecy and of all I have shown you is to tell about Jesus."‡

11 Then I saw heaven opened and a white horse standing there; and the One sitting on the horse was named "Faithful and True"—the One who justly punishes and makes war.

12 His eyes were like flames, and on His head were many crowns. A name was written on His forehead,§ and only He knew its meaning.

*literally, "he"; the exact antecedent is unclear.
†literally, "These are the true words of God."
‡literally, "the testimony of Jesus is the spirit of prophecy."
§implied.

13 He was clothed with garments dipped in blood, and His title was "The Word of God."*

14 The armies of heaven, dressed in finest linen, white and clean, followed Him on white horses.

15 In His mouth He held a sharp sword to strike down the nations; He ruled them with an iron grip; and He trod the winepress of the fierceness of the wrath of Almighty God.

16 On His robe and thigh were written this title: "KING OF KINGS AND LORD OF LORDS."

17 Then I saw an angel standing in the sunshine, shouting loudly to the birds, "Come! Gather together for the supper of the Great God!

18 Come and eat the flesh of kings, and captains, and great generals; of horses and riders; and of all humanity, both great and small, slave and free."

19 Then I saw the Evil Creature gathering the governments of the earth and their armies to fight against the One sitting on the horse and His army.

20 And the Evil Creature was captured, and with him the False Prophet,† who could do mighty miracles when the Evil Creature was present—miracles that deceived all who had accepted the Evil Creature's mark, and who worshiped his statue. Both of them—the Evil Creature and his False Prophet—were thrown alive into the Lake of Fire that burns with sulphur.

21 And their entire army was killed with the sharp sword in the mouth of the One riding the white horse, and all the birds of heaven were gorged with their flesh.

*literally, "The Logos," as in John 1:1—the ultimate method of God's revealing Himself to man.

†see chapter 13, verses 11-16.

CHAPTER 20

Then I saw an angel come down from heaven with the key to the bottomless pit and a heavy chain in his hand.

2 He seized the Dragon—that old Serpent, the Devil, Satan—and bound him in chains for 1,000 years,

3 And threw him into the bottomless pit, which he then shut and locked, so that he could not fool the nations any more until the thousand years were finished. Afterwards he would be released again for a little while.

4 Then I saw thrones, and sitting on them were those who had been given the right to judge. And I saw the souls of those who had been beheaded for their testimony about Jesus, for proclaiming the Word of God, and who had not worshiped the Creature or his statue, nor accepted his mark on their foreheads or their hands. They had come to life again and now they reigned with Christ for a thousand years.

5 This is the First Resurrection. (The rest of the dead did not come back to life until the thousand years had ended.)

6 Blessed and holy are those who share in the First Resurrection. For them the Second Death holds no terrors, for they will be priests of God and of Christ, and shall reign with Him a thousand years.

7 When the thousand years end, Satan will be let out of his prison.

8 He will go out to deceive the nations of the

world and gather them together, with Gog and Magog, for battle—a mighty host, numberless as sand along the shore.

9 They will go up across the broad plain of the earth and surround God's people and the beloved city of Jerusalem* on every side. But fire from God in heaven will flash down on the attacking armies and consume them.

10 Then the Devil who had betrayed them will again be thrown into the Lake of Fire burning with sulphur where the Creature and False Prophets are, and they will be tormented day and night forever and ever.

11 And I saw a great white throne and the One who sat upon it, from whose face the earth and sky fled away, but they found no place to hide.†

12 I saw the dead, great and small, standing before God; and The Books were opened, including the Book of Life. And the dead were judged according to the things written in The Books, each according to the deeds he had done.

13 The oceans surrendered the bodies buried in them; and the earth and the underworld gave up the dead in them. Each was judged according to his deeds.

14 And Death and Hell were thrown into the Lake of Fire. This is the Second Death—the Lake of Fire.

15 And if anyone's name was not found recorded in the Book of Life, he was thrown into the Lake of Fire.

*implied.
†literally, "There was no longer any place for them."

CHAPTER 21

Then I saw a new earth (with no oceans!) and a
new sky, for the present earth and sky had disappeared.
2 And I, John, saw the Holy City, the new Jerusalem, coming down from God out of heaven. It was
a glorious sight, beautiful as a bride at her wedding.
3 I heard a loud shout from the throne saying,
"Look, the home of God is now among men, and He
will live with them and they will be His people; yes,
God Himself will be among them.*
4 He will wipe away all tears from their eyes, and
there shall be no more death, or sorrow, or crying,
or pain. All of that has gone forever."
5 And the One sitting on the throne said, "See, I
am making all things new!" And then He said to
me, "Write this down, for what I tell you is trustworthy and true:
6 It is finished! I am the A and Z—the beginning
and the end. I will give to the thirsty the springs of
the Water of Life—as a gift!
7 Everyone who conquers will inherit all these
blessings, and I will be his God and he will be My
son.
8 But cowards who turn back from following Me,
and those who are unfaithful to Me, and murderers,
and those conversing with demons, and idol worshipers and all liars—their doom is in the Lake that
burns with fire and sulphur. This is the Second
Death."
9 Then one of the seven angels, who had emptied
the flasks containing the seven last plagues came

*Some manuscripts add, "and be their God."

and said to me, "Come with me and I will show you the bride, the Lamb's wife."

10 In a vision he took me to a towering mountain peak and from there I watched that wondrous city, the holy Jerusalem, descending out of the skies from God.

11 It was filled with the glory of God, and flashed and glowed like a precious gem, crystal clear like jasper.

12 Its walls were broad and high, with twelve gates guarded by twelve angels. And the names of the twelve tribes of Israel were written on the gates.

13 There were three gates on each side—north, south, east, and west.

14 The walls had twelve foundation stones, and on them were written the names of the twelve apostles of the Lamb.

15 The angel held in his hand a golden measuring stick to measure the city and its gates and walls.

16 When he measured it, he found it was a square as wide as it was long; in fact, it was in the form of a cube, for its height was exactly the same as its other dimensions—1500 miles each way.

17 Then he measured the thickness of the walls and found them to be 216 feet across! (The angel called out these measurements to me, using standard units.)*

18 The wall was made of jasper; the city itself was pure transparent gold, like glass!

*literally, "144 cubits by human measurements." A cubit was the average length of a man's arm—not an angel's! The angel used normal units of measurement that John could understand.

19 The foundation stones were inlaid with gems.
The first layer* with jasper;
The second with sapphire;
The third with chalcedony;
The fourth with emerald;
The fifth with sardonyx;

20 The sixth layer with sardus;
The seventh with chrysolite;
The eighth with beryl;
The ninth with topaz;
The tenth with chrysoprase;
The eleventh with jacinth;
The twelfth with amethyst.

21 The twelve gates were made of pearls—each
gate from a single pearl! And the main street was
pure transparent gold, like glass.

22 No temple could be seen in the city, for the
Lord God Almighty and the Lamb are worshiped
in it everywhere.†

23 And the city has no need of sun or moon to
light it, for the glory of God and of the Lamb il-
luminate it.

24 Its light will light the nations of the earth,
and the rulers of the world will come and bring their
glory to it.

25 Its gates never close: they stay open all day
long—and there is no night!

26 And the glory and honor of all the nations
shall be brought into it.

27 Nothing evil will be permitted in it—no one

*implied.
†literally, "are its temple."

immoral or dishonest—but only those whose names are written in the Lamb's Book of Life.

CHAPTER 22

And he pointed out to me a river of pure Water of Life, clear as crystal, flowing from the throne of God and the Lamb,

2 Coursing down the center of the main street. On each side of the river grew Trees* of Life, bearing twelve crops of fruit, with a fresh crop each month; the leaves were used for medicine to heal the nations.

3 There shall be nothing in the city which is evil; for the throne of God and of the Lamb will be there, and His servants will worship Him.

4 And they shall see His face; and His name shall be written on their foreheads.

5 And there will be no night there—no need for lamps or sun—for the Lord God will be their light; and they shall reign forever and ever.

* * * *

6, 7 Then the angel said to me, "These words are trustworthy and true: 'I am coming soon!'† God who tells His prophets what the future holds has sent His angel to tell you this will happen soon. Blessed are those who believe it and all else written in the scroll."

*literally, "the tree of life"—used here as a collective noun, implying plurality.

†or, "suddenly," "unexpectedly."

8 I, John, saw and heard all these things, and fell down to worship the angel who showed them to me;

9 But again he said, "No, don't do anything like that. I too am a servant of Jesus as you are, and as your brothers the prophets are, as well as all those who heed the truth stated in this Book. Worship God alone."

10 Then he instructed me, "Do not seal up what you have written, for the time of fulfillment is near.

11 And when that times comes, all doing wrong will do it more and more; the vile will become more vile; good men will be better; those who are holy will continue on in greater holiness."

12 "See, I am coming soon,* and My reward is with Me, to repay everyone according to the deeds he has done.

13 I am the A and Z, the Beginning and the End, the First and Last.

14 Blessed forever are all who are washing their robes, to have the right to enter in through the gates of the city, and to eat the fruit from the Tree of Life.

15 Outside the city are those who have strayed away from God, and the sorcerers and the immoral and murderers and idolaters, and all who love to lie, and do it.

16 I, Jesus, have sent My angel to you to tell the churches all these things. I am both David's Root and his Descendant. I am the bright Morning Star.

17 The Spirit and the bride say, 'Come.' Let each one who hears them say the same, 'Come.' Let the

*or, "suddenly," "unexpectedly."

thirsty one come—anyone who wants to; let him come and drink the Water of Life without charge.

18 And I solemnly declare to everyone who reads this book: if anyone adds anything to what is written here, God shall add to him the plagues described in this book.

19 And if anyone subtracts any part of these prophecies, God shall take away his share in the Tree of Life, and in the Holy City just described.

20 He who has said all these things declares: Yes, I am coming soon!"*

Amen! Come, Lord Jesus!

21 The grace of our Lord Jesus Christ be with you all. Amen!

*or, "suddenly," "unexpectedly."

Prophecies Concerning the Living Christ

Made and Fulfilled

Fulfilled prophecy is one of the strongest evidences that the Bible is the inspired Word of God. ". . . the Spirit of Christ which was in the them [the prophets] did signify, when it testified beforehand the sufferings of Christ, and the glory that should follow" (1 Peter 1:11).

The Scripture passages quoted here are all concerned with Jesus Christ, His birth, life, death, resurrection and ascension. This theme is representative of other great themes of the Bible, showing the supernatural origin of the authorship of God's Word. (Prophecies are in regular type, fulfillments in italic type.)

Therefore the Lord himself shall give you a sign; Behold a virgin shall conceive, and bear a son, and shall call his name Immanuel. (Isaiah 7:14)

Now the birth of Jesus Christ was on this wise: When as his mother Mary was espoused to Joseph, before they came together, she was found with child of the Holy Ghost . . . Now all this was done, that it might be fulfilled which was spoken of the Lord by the prophet, saying, Behold, a virgin shall be with child, and shall bring forth a son, and they shall call his name Immanuel, which being interpreted is, God with us. (Matthew 1:18,22,23)

And I will bless them that bless thee [Abraham], and curse him that curseth thee: and in thee shall all families of the earth be blessed. (Genesis 12:3)
And I will make thy [Isaac's] seed to multiply as the stars of heaven, and will give unto thy seed all these countries; and in thy seed shall all the nations of the earth be blessed. (Genesis 26:4)
And thy [Jacob's] seed shall be as the dust of the earth; and thou shalt spread abroad to the west, and to the east, and to the north, and to the south: and in thee and in thy seed shall all the families of the earth be blessed. (Genesis 28:14)
And there shall come forth a rod out of the stem of Jesse,

and a Branch shall grow out of his roots: (Isaiah 11:1)
And thine [David's] house and thy kingdom shall be established for ever before thee: thy throne shall be established forever. (2 Samuel 7:16)
Then I will establish the throne of thy [Solomon's] Kingdom upon Israel for ever, as I promised to David thy father, saying, There shall not fail thee a man upon the throne of Israel. (1 Kings 9:5)

Abraham begat Isaac; and Isaac begat Jacob; and Jacob begat Judas and his brethren; . . . And Jesse begat David the king; and David the king begat Solomon of her that had been the wife of Urias. (Matthew 1:2,6)

But thou, Bethlehem Ephratah, though thou be little among the thousands of Judah, yet out of thee shall he come forth unto me that is to be ruler in Israel; whose goings forth have been from of old, from everlasting. (Micah 5:2)

And Joseph also went up from Galilee, out of the city of Nazareth, into Judea, unto the city of David, which is called Bethlehem, (because he was of the house and lineage of David,) to be taxed with Mary his espoused wife, being great with child. And so it was, that, while they were there, the days were accomplished that she should be delivered. (Luke 2:4-6)

The Lord thy God will raise up unto thee a Prophet from the midst of thee, of thy brethren, like unto me; unto him ye shall hearken. (Deuteronomy 18:15)

Philip findeth Nathanael, and saith unto him, We have found him, of whom Moses in the law, and the prophets, did write, Jesus of Nazareth, the son of Joseph (John 1:45)
Then those men, when they had seen the miracle that Jesus did, said, This is of a truth that Prophet that should come into the world. (John 6:14)
For Moses truly said unto the fathers, A Prophet shall the Lord your God raise up unto you of your brethren, like unto me; him shall ye hear in all things whatsoever he shall say unto you. And it shall come to pass, that

every soul, which will not hear that Prophet, shall be destroyed from among the people. Yea, and all the prophets from Samuel and those that follow after, as many as have spoken, have likewise foretold of these days. (Acts 3:22-24)

The Spirit of the Lord God is upon me; because the Lord hath anointed me to preach good tidings unto the meek; he hath sent me to bind up the broken-hearted, to proclaim liberty to the captives, and the opening of the prison to them that are bound; to proclaim the acceptable year of the Lord. (Isaiah 61:1,2a)

And he came to Nazareth, where he had been brought up: and, as his custom was, he went into the synagogue on the sabbath day, and stood up for to read. And there was delivered unto him the book of the prophet Esaias. And when he had opened the book, he found the place where it was written, The Spirit of the Lord is upon me, because he hath anointed me to preach the gospel to the poor; he hath sent me to heal the broken-hearted, to preach deliverance to the captives, and recovering of sight to the blind, to set at liberty them that are bruised, To preach the acceptable year of the Lord. And he closed the book, and he gave it again to the minister, and sat down. And the eyes of all them that were in the synagogue were fastened on him. And he began to say unto them, This day is this Scripture fulfilled in your ears. (Luke 4:16-21)

The sun shall no more go down; neither shall thy moon withdraw itself: for the Lord shall be thine everlasting light, and the days of thy mourning shall be ended. (Isaiah 60:20)

Then spake Jesus again unto them, saying, I am the light of the world: he that followeth me shall not walk in darkness, but shall have the light of life. (John 8:12)

Then the eyes of the blind shall be opened, and the ears of the deaf be unstopped. Then shall the lame man leap as a hart, and the tongue of the dumb sing. (Isaiah 35: 5,6a)

Jesus answered and said unto them, Go and show John again those things which ye do hear and see: The blind receive their sight, and the lame walk, the lepers are cleansed, and the deaf hear, the dead are raised up, and the poor have the gospel preached to them. (Matthew 11:4,5)

I will open my mouth in a parable: I will utter dark sayings of old. (Psalm 78:2)

All these things spake Jesus unto the multitude in parables; and without a parable spake he not unto them: That it might be fulfilled which was spoken by the prophet, saying, I will open my mouth in parables; I will utter things which have been kept secret from the foundation of the world. (Matthew 13:34,35)

Rejoice greatly, oh My people! Shout with joy! For look — your King is coming! He is the Righteous One, the Victor! yet He is lowly, riding on a donkey's colt! (Zechariah 9:9 Living Prophecies)

And they brought the colt to Jesus, and cast their garments on him; and he sat upon him. And many spread their garments on the way: and others cut down branches off the trees, and strawed them in the way. And they that went before, and they that followed, cried, saying, Hosanna; Blessed is he that cometh in the name of the Lord. (Mark 11:7-9)

And I said unto them, If ye think good, give me my price; and if not, forbear. So they weighed for my price thirty pieces of silver. And the Lord said unto me, Cast it unto the potter: a goodly price that I was prized at of them. And I took the thirty pieces of silver, and cast them to the potter in the house of the Lord. (Zechariah 11:12-13)

Then Judas, which had betrayed him, when he saw that he was condemned, repented himself, and brought again the thirty pieces of silver to the chief priests and elders . . . And the chief priests took the silver pieces, and said, It is not lawful for to put them into the treasury, because it is the price of blood. And they took counsel, and bought with them the potter's field, to bury strangers in. (Matthew 27:3,6,7)

"Awake, oh Sword, against My Shepherd, the man who is my associate and equal," says the Lord of Hosts. "Strike down the Shepherd and the sheep will scatter; but I will come back and comfort and care for the lambs." (Zechariah 13:7 Living Prophecies)

But all this was done, that the Scriptures of the prophets might be fulfilled. Then all the disciples forsook him, and fled. (Matthew 26:56)

They shall smite the judge of Israel with a rod upon the cheek. (Micah 5:1b)

And when they had blindfolded him, they struck him on the face, and asked him, saying, Prophesy, who is it that smote thee? (Luke 22:64)

He was oppressed, and he was afflicted, yet he opened not his mouth: he is brought as a lamb to the slaughter, and as a sheep before her shearers is dumb, so he openeth not his mouth. (Isaiah 53:7)

And when he was accused of the chief priests and elders, he answered nothing. Then said Pilate unto him, Hearest thou not how many things they witness against thee? And he answered him to never a word; insomuch that the governor marveled greatly. (Matthew 27:12-14)

All they that see me laugh me to scorn: they shoot out the lip, they shake the head, saying, He trusted on the Lord that he would deliver him: let him deliver him, seeing he delighted in him. (Psalm 22:7-8)

And they that passed by reviled him, wagging their heads, and saying, Thou that destroyest the temple, and buildest it in three days, save thyself. If thou be the Son of God, come down from the cross. He trusted in God; let him deliver him now, if he will have him: for he said, I am the Son of God. (Matthew 27:39,40,42,43)

Surely he hath borne our griefs, and carried our sorrows: yet we did esteem him stricken, smitten of God, and afflicted. But he was wounded for our transgressions, he was bruised for our iniquities: the chastisement of our peace was upon him; and with his stripes we are healed. All we like sheep have gone astray; we have turned every one to his own way; and the Lord hath laid on him the iniquity of us all. (Isaiah 53:4-6)

For Christ also hath once suffered for sins, the just for the unjust, that he might bring us to God, being put to death in the flesh, but quickened by the Spirit. (1 Peter 3:18)

They gave me also gall for my meat; and in my thirst they gave me vinegar to drink. (Psalm 69:21)

They gave him vinegar to drink mingled with gall: and when he had tasted thereof, he would not drink. (Matthew 27:34)

My God, my God, why hast thou forsaken me? (Psalm 22:1a)

And at the ninth hour Jesus cried with a loud voice, saying, Éloi, Éloi lama sabachthani? which is, being interpreted, My God, my God, why hast thou forsaken me? (Mark 15:34)

They put my garments among them, and cast lots upon my vesture. (Psalm 22:18)

Then the soldiers, when they had crucified Jesus, took his garments, and made four parts, to every soldier a part; and also his coat: now the coat was without seam, woven from the top throughout. They said therefore among themselves, Let us not rend it, but cast lots for it, whose it shall be: (John 19:23,24a)

The assembly of the wicked have inclosed me; they pierced my hands and my feet. (Psalm 22:16b)

And they crucified him. (Matthew 27:35a)

He keepeth all his bones: not one of them is broken. (Psalm 34:20)

But when they came to Jesus, and saw that he was dead already, they brake not his legs. (John 19:33)

And he made his grave with the wicked, and with the rich in his death. (Isaiah 53:9a)

When the even was come, there came a rich man of Arimathea, named Joseph, who also himself was Jesus' disciple: He went to Pilate, and begged the body of Jesus. Then Pilate commanded the body to be delivered. And when Joseph had taken the body, he wrapped it in a clean linen cloth, and laid it in his own new tomb, which he had hewn out in the rock. (Matthew 27:57-60a)

For thou wilt not leave my soul in hell; neither wilt thou suffer thine Holy One to see corruption. (Psalm 16:10)

And he saith unto them, Be not affrighted: ye seek Jesus of Nazareth, which was crucified: he is risen; he is not here: behold the place where they laid him. (Mark 16:6)

Thou hast ascended on high, thou hast led captivity captive. (Psalm 68:18a)

And when he had spoken these things, while they beheld, he was taken up; and a cloud received him out of their sight. (Acts 1:9)

Therefore thus saith the Lord God, Behold, I lay in Zion for a foundation stone, a tried stone, a precious corner stone, a sure foundation: he that believeth shall not make haste. (Isaiah 28:16)
The stone which the builders refused is become the head stone of the corner. (Psalm 118:22)

Wherefore also it is contained in the Scripture, Behold, I lay in Zion a chief corner stone, elect, precious: and he that believeth on him shall not be confounded. Unto you therefore which believe he is precious: but unto them which be disobedient, the stone which the builders disallowed, the same is made the head of the corner. (1 Peter 2:6,7)

Prophecies Concerning the Living Christ
Yet to be Fulfilled

The prophecies made about Christ's first appearance have come true, and by faith we believe those concerning His return will also come true.

This is the "blessed hope" (Titus 2:13) which should be proclaimed throughout the world.

May these Scripture passages encourage and stimulate everyone to a dedication to Christ and His service.

And when he had spoken these things, while they beheld, he was taken up; and a cloud received him out of their sight. And while they looked steadfastly toward heaven as he went up, behold, two men stood by them in white apparel; which also said, Ye men of Galilee, why stand ye gazing up into heaven? this same Jesus, which is taken up from you into heaven, shall so come in like manner as ye have seen him go into heaven. (Acts 1:9-11)

Let not your heart be troubled: ye believe in God, believe also in me. In my Father's house are many mansions: if it were not so, I would have told you. I go to prepare a place for you. And if I go and prepare a place for you, I will come again, and receive you unto myself; that where I am, there ye may be also. And whither I go ye know, and the way ye know. Thomas saith unto him, Lord, we know not whither thou goest; and how can we know the way? Jesus saith unto him, I am the way, the truth, and the life: no man cometh unto the Father, but by me. (John 14:1-6)

Behold, I show you a mystery; We shall not all sleep, but we shall all be changed, in a moment, in the twinkling of an eye, at the last trump: for the trumpet shall sound, and the dead shall be raised incorruptible, and we shall be changed. (1 Corinthians 15:51,52)

But I would not have you to be ignorant, brethren, concerning them which are asleep, that ye sorrow not, even as others which have no hope. For if we believe that Jesus died and rose again, even so them also which sleep in Jesus will God bring with him. For this we say unto you by the word of the Lord, that we which are alive and remain unto the coming of the Lord shall not prevent [precede] them which are asleep. For the Lord himself shall descend from heaven with a shout, with the voice of the archangel, and with the trump of God: and the dead in Christ shall rise first: Then we which are alive and remain shall be caught up together with them in the clouds, to meet the Lord in the air: and so shall we ever be with the Lord. Wherefore comfort one another with these words. (1 Thessalonians 4:13-18)

Looking for that blessed hope, and the glorious appearing of the great God and our Saviour Jesus Christ: (Titus 2:13)

Immediately after the tribulation of those days shall the sun be darkened, and the moon shall not give her light, and the stars shall fall from heaven, and the powers of the heavens shall be shaken: And then shall appear the sign of the Son of Man in heaven: and then shall all the tribes of the earth mourn, and they shall see the Son of man coming in the clouds of heaven with power and great glory. And he shall send his angels with a great sound of a trumpet, and they shall gather together his elect from the four winds, from one end of heaven to the other . . . But of that day and hour knoweth no man, no, not the angels of heaven, but my Father only. But as the days of Noe were, so shall also the coming of the Son of man be. For as in the days that were before the flood they were eating and drinking, marrying and giving in marriage, until the day that Noe entered into the ark, and knew not until the flood came, and took them all away; so shall also the coming of the Son of man be. Then shall two be in the field; the one shall be taken, and the other left Two women shall be grinding at the mill; the one shall be taken, and the other left. Watch therefore; for ye know not what hour your Lord doth come. (Matthew 24:29-31, 36-42)

Repent ye therefore, and be converted, that your sins may be blotted out, when the times of refreshing shall come from the presence of the Lord; And he shall send

Jesus Christ, which before was preached unto you: Whom the heaven must receive until the times of restitution of all things, which God hath spoken by the mouth of all his holy prophets since the world began. (Acts 3: 19-21)

And as it is appointed unto men once to die, but after this the judgment: So Christ was once offered to bear the sins of many; and unto them that look for him shall he appear the second time without sin unto salvation. (Hebrews 9:27,28)

Beloved, now are we the sons of God, and it doth not yet appear what we shall be: but we know that, when he shall appear, we shall be like him; for we shall see him as he is. (1 John 3:2)

But of the times and the seasons, brethren, ye have no need that I write unto you. For yourselves know perfectly that the day of the Lord so cometh as a thief in the night. For when they shall say, Peace and safety; then sudden destruction cometh upon them, as travail upon a woman with child; and they shall not escape. But ye, brethren, are not in darkness, that that day should overtake you as a thief. (1 Thessalonians 5:1-4)

I saw in the night visions, and, behold, one like the Son of man came with the clouds of heaven, and came to the Ancient of days, and they brought him near before him. And there was given him dominion, and glory, and a kingdom, that all people, nations, and languages, should serve him: his dominion is an everlasting dominion, which shall not pass away, and his kingdom that which shall not be destroyed. (Daniel 7:13-14)

Jesus saith unto him, Thou hast said: nevertheless I say unto you, Hereafter shall ye see the Son of man sitting on the right hand of power, and coming in the clouds of heaven. (Matthew 26:64)

For we must all appear before the judgment seat of Christ; that every one may receive the things done in his body, according to that he hath done, whether it be good or bad. (2 Corinthians 5:10)

For unto us a child is born, unto us a son is given: and the government shall be upon his shoulder: and his name shall be called Wonderful, Counselor, The mighty God, The everlasting Father, The Prince of Peace. Of the increase of his government and peace there shall be no end, upon the throne of David, and upon his kingdom, to order it, and to establish it with judgment and with justice from henceforth even for ever. The zeal of the Lord of hosts will perform this. (Isaiah 9:6,7)

He shall have dominion also from sea to sea, and from the river unto the ends of the earth . . . Yea, all kings shall fall down before him: all nations shall serve him. (Psalm 72:8,11)

See! He is arriving surrounded by clouds; and every eye shall see Him . . . (Revelation 1:7a Living Prophecies)

I saw the dead, great and small, standing before God; and The Books were opened, including the Book of Life. And the dead were judged according to the things written in The Books, each according to the deeds he had done . . . And if anyone's name was not found recorded in the Book of Life, he was thrown into the Lake of Fire. (Revelation 20:12,15 Living Prophecies)

I heard a loud shout from the throne saying, "Look, the home of God is now among men, and He will live with them and they will be His people; yes, God Himself will be among them. He will wipe away all tears from their eyes, and there shall be no more death, or sorrow, or crying, or pain. All of that has gone forever." And the One sitting on the throne said, "See, I am making all things new!" And then He said to me, "Write this down, for what I tell you is trustworthy and true: It is finished! I am the A and Z – the beginning and the end. I will give to the thirsty the springs of the Water of Life – as a gift!" (Revelation 21:3-6 Living Prophecies)

He who has said all these things declares: "Yes, I am coming soon!" Amen! Come, Lord Jesus! (Revelation 22:20 Living Prophecies)

* * *

But these are written, that ye might believe that Jesus is the Christ, the Son of God; and that believing ye might have life through his name. (John 20:31)

Time-Line Comparisons

	Date (B.C.)*	*Event*	*Prophet*	*King of Israel*	*King of Judah*
	1004			David, King of United Israelite Kingdom	
	965			Solomon, King of United Israelite Kingdom	
	927	Invasion of Shishak, King of Egypt			
	926	Division of the Monarchy		Jeroboam I	Rehoboam
	910				Abijah
	908				Asa
	907			Nadab	
	906			Baasha	
Assyria as world power	884	Ashurnasirpal, II King of Assyria			
	883			Elah	
	882			Zimri	
				Omri	
	876				Jehoshaphat
	871			Ahab	
	865		Elijah		
	859	Shalmaneser III, King of Assyria			
	852			Ahaziah	
	851			Joram	
	850				Jehoram
	845		Elisha		
	841			Jehu	Ahaziah
					Athaliah
	840	Probable period of Homer			
	836				Joash
	814			Jehoahaz	
	810	Adad-Nirari III, King of Assyria			
	800	Foundation of Carthage	Joel		
	798			Jehoash	
	797				Amaziah
	793			Jeroboam II	
	791				Uzziah

Assyria as world power

Date	Event	Prophets	Kings of Israel	Kings of Judah
776	First Olympic Games			
775		Jonah		
760		Amos		
753			Zechariah	
752			Shallum	
751			Menahem	Jotham
750		Hosea		
745	Tiglath-Pileser III, King of Assyria			
741			Pekahiah	
740			Pekah	
736				Ahaz
732	Damascus falls to Assyria			
731			Hoshea	
729				Hezekiah
727	Shalmaneser V of Assyria besieges Samaria			
725	Coinage in Lydia and Ionia	Isaiah		
722	Fall of Samaria to Assyria			
705	Sennacherib, King of Assyria			
700		Micah		
696				Manasseh
689	Taharka, King of Ethiopia			
674	Assyrian occupation of Egypt			
669	Ashurbanipal, King of Assyria			
661		Nahum		
660	Zarathustra (Zoroaster)			
660	Entrance of Mongols into Japan			
652	Gyges, King of Lydia			
641				Amon
639	Fall of Susa and of Elam			Josiah
630	Laws of Lycurgus at Sparta			
626		Zephaniah		
625		Habakkuk		
620	Laws of Draco at Athens			
614	Assyria falls to the Medes			
612	Nineveh, capital of Assyria, falls			
609		Jeremiah		Jehoahaz
608				Jehoiakim
605	Nebuchadnezzar II, King of Babylonia	Daniel		
604-531	Lao-tzu, Chinese philosopher			

*Approximate

Time-Line Comparisons

	Date* (B.C.)	Event	Prophet	King of Israel	King of Judah
Babylonian rule	600	Foundation of Marseilles			
			Ezekial		
	599	Mahavira Jnatiputra, founder of Jainism			
	598		Jeremiah		Jehoiachin
	597				Zedekiah
	594	Laws of Solon at Athens			
	590	Second Temple of Artemis at Ephesus			
	587	Fall of Jerusalem to Babylonia			
	586		Obadiah		
	580	Aesop of Samos, fabulist			
	570	Croesus, King of Lydia			
	563-483	Buddha			
	558	Carthage conquers Sicily and Corsica			
	556-539	Nabonidus			
	551-478	Confucius			
Persian rule	529-500	Pythagoras, philosopher			
	525	Persian conquest of Egypt			
	521	Darius I, King of Persia			
	520	Building of second temple at Jerusalem	Haggai		
	518		Zechariah		
	516	Temple complete			
	509	Roman Republic established			
	490	Defeat of the Persians at Marathon			
	485	Xerxes I, King of Persia			
	476	Esther is Queen			
	475		Malachi		
	465	Artaxerxes I, King of Persia			
	460-429	Age of Pericles in Greece; Socrates, Plato			
	458	Rebuilding Jerusalem	Ezra		
	447	Building of the Parthenon is begun			
	445	Rebuilding Jerusalem	Nehemiah		
	432	Sophocles			
	423	Darius II, King of Persia			